CONTENTS

Acknowledgments

A piece of work like this draws on the input of numerous people and organisations. Without the generous financial support of PricewaterhouseCoopers LLP and the South East Counties this work would not have been possible. Many of the detailed issues arising from the Commission's work were explored as part of a series of working papers and public seminars. These involved a number of people who were not Commissioners but who gave up a considerable amount of their time. Our thanks go to: Chris Lawrence-Pietroni, Keith Mitchell, Nick Jones, Andrew Thurley, Katerina Coumis, Matthew Taylor, Glen Bramley, Peter Hall, Susan Fainstein, Robert Kloosterman, Cindy Warwick, Chris Hewett, Steve Cook, Elliot Robertson, Paul Hackett and Peter Headicar.

At the ippr, many others have given support, expert advice, contributed to putting together events and publications as well as helping to disseminate our research. We would particularly like to thank Rachel O'Brien, Howard Reed, John Schwartz, Matt Jackson, John Adams, Tim Gosling, Dermot Finch, Max Nathan and Jim Bennett (on secondment from Shelter). We were also helped by Erica Hope who was an intern at ippr over the course of the Commission.

Whilst we have benefited a great deal from the forementioned people it should be noted that the views expressed in this report are solely those of the Commissioners.

7 Day

AINABLE
TH EAST

University of Plymouth Library

Subject to status this item may be renewed
via your Voyager account

http://voyager.plymouth.ac.uk

Exeter tel: (01392) 475049
Exmouth tel: (01395) 255331
Plymouth tel: (01752) 232323

ippr

The **Institute for Public Policy Research** (ippr) is the UK's leading progressive think tank and was established in 1988. Its role is to bridge the political divide between the social democratic and liberal traditions, the intellectual divide between academia and the policy-making establishment and the cultural divide between government and civil society. It is first and foremost a research institute, aiming to provide innovative and credible policy solutions. Its work, the questions its research poses and the methods it uses are driven by the belief that the journey to a good society is one that places social justice, democratic participation and economic and environmental sustainability at its core.

For further information you can contact ippr's external affairs department on info@ippr.org, you can view our website at www.ippr.org and you can buy our books from Central Books on 0845 458 9910 or email ippr@centralbooks.com.

The Commissioners and the Secretariat

The Commissioners

Sir Sandy Bruce-Lockhart OBE (Commission Chairman) – Leader, Kent County Council and Chairman, Local Government Association

Nicholas Boles – Director, Policy Exchange

Dr Valerie Ellis – Member of the Sustainable Development Commission

Robert Douglas – Deputy Chair, South East England Development Agency (SEEDA)

Chris Huhne – MP for Eastleigh

Nick Pearce – Director, ippr

Sue Regan – former Director of Policy, Shelter

Cllr Dame Jane Roberts OBE – Leader, Camden Council

Alistair Rose – Regional Chairman for the South East, PricewaterhouseCoopers LLP

Richard Shaw – Chief Executive, Surrey County Council

Cllr Nick Skellett – Leader, Surrey County Council and Chair, South East England Regional Assembly (SEERA)

Baroness Barbara Young – Chief Executive, Environment Agency

The ippr Secretariat

Julie Foley, Senior Research Fellow (Commission Secretary)

Louise Every, Research Assistant

Tony Grayling, Associate Director

Peter Robinson, Associate Director

Nathan Sansom, Research Assistant

Anthony Vigor, Research Fellow

Commission working papers produced by ippr

'Going for Growth: Comparing the South East's Economic Performance'
Peter Robinson, ippr, 18 October 2004.

'The Problems of Success: Reconciling Economic Growth and Quality of Life in the South East'
Julie Foley, ippr, 22 November 2004.

'Keeping the South East Moving'
Julie Foley, Nathan Sansom and Tony Grayling, ippr, 15 February 2005.

'Managing Water Resources and Flood Risk in the South East'
Louise Every and Julie Foley, ippr, 21 March 2005.

'Meeting Housing Needs in the South East'
Anthony Vigor and Peter Robinson, ippr, 7 April 2005.

All the above working papers can be downloaded from ippr's website: www.ippr.org

Commission seminars

As part of the Commission's work we held the following public seminars:

13 September 2004.
'Going for Growth: Comparing the South East's Economic Performance with Other Regions'
Alistair Rose, Regional Chairman for the South East, PricewaterhouseCoopers LLP (chair)
Peter Robinson, Senior Economist, ippr; Robert Douglas, Deputy Chair, South East England
Development Agency (SEEDA); and Philip Cox, Head of ODPM/DTI/HM Treasury Regional
Performance Public Service Agreement, Office of the Deputy Prime Minister (ODPM).

20 September 2004.
'Making Quality of Life Count in the South East'
Nick Pearce, Director, ippr (chair)
Julie Foley, Senior Research Fellow, ippr; Paul Bevan, Chief Executive, South East England
Regional Assembly (SEERA); Jill Rutter, Director of Strategy and Sustainable Development,
Department for Environment, Food and Rural Affairs (DEFRA); and Peter Madden, Head of
Environment Policy, Environment Agency.

22 October 2004.
'Keeping the South East Moving'
Richard Shaw, Chief Executive, Oxfordshire County Council (chair)
Nathan Sansom, Researcher, ippr; Dr Peter Headicar, Reader in Transport, Oxford Brookes
University; and Andy Roberts, Director of Transport, Government Office for the South East
(GOSE).

30 November 2004.
'Managing Floods and Droughts: Water in the South East'
Julie Foley, Senior Research Fellow, ippr (chair)
Louise Every, Researcher, ippr; Barbara Young, Chief Executive, Environment Agency;
Elizabeth Wilson, Principal Lecturer in Environmental Planning, Oxford Brookes University;
and Graham Setterfield, independent water consultant.

10 December 2004.
Is the South East a Mega-City Region?
Sir Sandy Bruce-Lockhart OBE, Leader of Kent County Council and Chairman of the Local
Government Association (LGA) (chair)
Professor Sir Peter Hall, Director, Institute of Community Studies; Professor Robert
Kloosterman, Professor of Economic Geography and Planning, University of Amsterdam; and
Susan Fainstein, Professor of Urban Planning, University of Columbia.

19 January 2005.
'A Home for Everyone? Housing Need in the South East of England'
Sue Regan, Director of Policy, Shelter (chair)
Anthony Vigor, Research Fellow, ippr; Glen Bramley, Professor of Urban Studies, Heriot-Watt University; Simon Ridley, Head of Housing and Urban Policy Team, HM Treasury; and Nick Townsend, Group Legal Director, Wilson Bowden.

Foreword

Sir Sandy Bruce-Lockhart OBE, Commission Chairman

In July 2004, the ippr established the Commission on Sustainable Development in the South East, which has been one of its flagship research projects during 2004-05.

To forge consensus around some of the challenging issues facing a prosperous, high growth region like the South East, the ippr brought together Commissioners from the business, voluntary and environmental sectors with cross-party political representatives from the South East and London. The Commission began its work at a time of great uncertainty about the future direction of the South East – the Government had published its Sustainable Communities Plan which set out controversial proposals for new growth areas across the South East region. In particular, there was a great deal of debate about the increased housing targets for the South East counties.

The South East is made up of the seven counties to the south, south west and south east of London. With England becoming increasingly London-centric, and London growing as a world city, the South East position next to the capital is of increasing importance both in economic terms and as a green hinterland to London with its attractive countryside, environment and heritage.

Over the last few years there has been growing concern over the environmental and social pressures facing the region. Whilst it is true that the South East is one of the most successful regions in the UK, and indeed Europe, this success does not yet benefit everyone living in the region. There remain stark disparities across the South East and entrenched areas of deprivation, particularly along the South East coast, with low employment rates amongst disadvantaged groups.

A year after the Commission started, the Labour Government was elected for a third term. The Commission's final report therefore comes at a time when an injection of new ideas and a new direction for government policy is needed.

A Commission of this kind proves that there is much consensus around the need for a new approach to growth in the South East, driven not simply by the objective of maximising economic growth but by 'quality of life' concerns.

During the year, the Commissioners, who had started with widely differing views, found that with the benefit of impressive research papers produced by the ippr, their views had coalesced. This was particularly evident when the Commissioners concluded that the goal for the South East should not be raising Gross Domestic Product (GDP) in total, but rather GDP per head and prosperity per household. The Commission concluded that this could be best driven forward by helping more people who are economically inactive back into work, so that they can lead more independent and fulfilling lives.

The key to reducing intra-regional disparities will be policies that are successful at lowering the number of people who are economically inactive in the South East. However, improving employment rates is essential not only to narrow disparities within the South East, but also to reduce disparities between regions. A national, short term regional policy based on moving economic activity around the country will not work. There is a growing appreciation within the South East that we have a vested interest in boosting employment and skills not only in our region, but also in the less prosperous regions. This will help ease population and housing pressures on the Greater South East and will make it easier for us to manage some of the problems of success which threaten our environment and quality of life.

What has become clear is that the Government will find it difficult to deliver on its aspirations of high growth in housebuilding without a significant increase in public spending on public transport, especially better rail services, infrastructure funding for roads and community facilities as well as flood risk management. This must be combined with investment to deliver housebuilding on the large number of difficult brownfield sites that have been available for some while.

Across the South East, a more local approach to planning and development needs to be taken. Local authorities should be encouraged to take a central role in driving regeneration. If local authorities were given greater responsibility, and if infrastructure funding was matched to the delivery of housing, then local councils would have the incentive and public support to ensure delivery of local housing needs. Alongside this there needs to be better co-ordination of policy-making and delivery, both within the South East and across the Greater South East area.

Maintaining a high quality of life in the South East will require the co-operation of all sectors of society. The challenge facing regions like ours is to identify ways of encouraging and enabling individuals and firms to consume resources more efficiently and produce less waste and pollution. Part of this will involve developing new ways of paying for services to encourage more sustainable consumption choices.

I would like to offer my sincere thanks to all the Commissioners for their time and commitment in producing what I believe is an excellent and robust report. Whilst not every Commissioner may agree with all the recommendations in this report, all agree with the key arguments put forward. I would also like to pass on my gratitude to the South East Counties and PricewaterhouseCoopers for supporting the Commission's work.

Last but not least, I would like to thank Julie Foley and the ippr team who have provided the Secretariat to the Commission, and have supported our work with high quality, independent research and with the ippr's own expertise and professionalism.

Executive summary: Sustainable development in the South East

The Commission's goal is for the South East to maintain its economic success and its position as one of Europe's most prosperous regions, while at the same time enhancing its environment and improving the wellbeing and quality of life of all its citizens. The Commission shall take into account the position of the South East with regards to London as a world city and as the frontier to mainland Europe, as well as considering the UK's inter-regional disparities.

The South East is one of the most prosperous regions in the UK and in Europe. It has a strong economy and provides a high standard of living for most of its citizens. But it is also a victim of its own success. As a high growth region, it suffers from traffic congestion and pollution. There is a shortage of affordable housing in the South East with rising numbers of people living in temporary accommodation. The environment is under pressure. As the world's climate changes, the South East will experience more frequent water shortages during the summer months and more floods during the winter months.

The South East faces a fundamental choice. Either it carries on down the path of traditional economic growth, with higher levels of congestion, worsening air quality and greater pressures on the natural environment. Or it chooses a sustainable future and takes the path of smarter growth – maintaining its economic prosperity but spreading the benefits to all its citizens, protecting the environment and safeguarding the region for future generations. This report shows how the South East can choose smart growth and a sustainable future. It argues that:

■ prosperity cannot simply be measured in terms of economic output – quality of life and protection of the environment must be factored in;

■ boosting the economic performance of the less prosperous regions in the UK will make it easier for the South East to cope with the problems that current levels of relative economic prosperity pose;

■ wellbeing should be shared across the South East – those parts of the region and its people that have fallen behind should be included in the South East's success through a focus on increasing employment rates;

■ sustainable development requires new investment in the region's infrastructure – particularly in its transport, affordable housing and flood defences;

■ with investment must come changes in behaviour – we must learn to value the region's environment and be prepared to pay to protect it through pricing mechanisms like road user charging; and

■ to make progress, the South East needs a new democratic settlement, with a locally sensitive approach to planning and delivering new development, reforms to regional governance and greater co-ordination of planning across the Greater South East.

The Commission's key findings

The South East's inter-relationship with London, the rest of the UK and Europe

South East's economic performance

■ The economic performance of the South East compares well with what are generally regarded as the EU's most prosperous substantive regions containing all the well known centres of commerce in Europe outside of London and Paris.

■ There is broad consensus in the South East for continued economic growth in the region at about current levels. No-one in the region appears to be arguing for an increased rate of economic growth in the South East.

South East's inter-relationship with London

■ Many people move in and out of the capital at certain points in their lives to meet their aspirations for different forms of housing. Those people moving out of London into the South East tend to be families and older people. The South East is also indirectly affected by London's attraction of international migrants, which adds pressure to the housing market in the capital that then results in an out-migration 'cascade effect' increasing population pressures in the South East.

■ Meeting London's future housing needs will be challenging. A debate needs to be had about whether neighbouring regions like the South East can be expected to fill the gap if London is unable to meet its own housing needs. London also has to address how it will accommodate a greater population probably at higher densities.

■ It is unclear how much of London's water demand is met from water resources in the South East. It is unknown what impact London's future water needs could have on water availability and, to a lesser extent, the capacity of sewerage and drainage systems in the South East.

South East comparisons with the rest of the UK

■ Households in the South East consume more water per capita compared to the other English regions. Yet the region has some of the lowest water metering rates in England and Wales.

■ The South East's travel patterns are not greatly different compared to the other English regions. However, the South East has high levels of car ownership and motorists in the South East drive more miles by car compared to most other English regions.

- Compared to other parts of the UK, the South East is likely to experience the highest annual damage to residential and commercial developments from flooding over future decades.

- The South East is probably the only UK region with an above average growth rate in output per head. In contrast, the North East and Wales are the two UK regions with a below average growth rate.

Inter-regional disparities

- Despite the Government having a target to reduce disparities between regions, it has acknowledged that inter-regional disparities are in fact getting worse. The Government should introduce a new Public Service Agreement target for addressing regional disparities in economic performance:

Over the long term reduce the persistent gap in output per head between the UK's regions by concentrating effort on increasing the growth rate in the lagging regions (with a particular focus on employment).

- For the South East region this would mean voicing support for the efforts of the less prosperous regions, individually and collectively, to tackle their economic problems and particularly their relatively low employment rates. The emphasis here is not on what could be characterised as old fashioned policy instruments designed to move economic activity around the country, but policies to improve employment and skills within the less prosperous regions.

Addressing disparities within the South East

Employment, skills and housing

- Although the South East is one of the most prosperous regions in the UK and EU, there are serious economic disparities within the region especially along parts of the south coast. There are also low employment rates among disadvantaged groups such as the long term sick and disabled.

- The Government has a target for an 80 per cent employment rate for all adults aged 16-64 by around 2020. In the South East the current overall employment rate is 77 per cent. Meeting the Government's target will require specific attention to be given to increasing the labour market participation of those people who are economically inactive.

- The labour market in the South East is relatively tight but it is not overheating. Skills shortages and skills gaps do not seem to be a bigger problem in the South East than in other English regions and are not getting worse. The shortages that do exist are surprisingly widely spread across both higher and lower skilled occupations.

- The South East is already able to draw on the most highly qualified labour from national and, indeed, international markets. Improvements in skills attainment within the region will help meet the demand for more highly qualified labour. There needs to be a balance between in-migration and mobilising the labour supply within the region to meet future labour demand.

- The challenge facing the South East is to increase employment rates in its less prosperous areas and among older workers and groups disadvantaged in the labour market. If it can meet this challenge, significantly higher levels of housing growth – above those set out in the *South East Plan: Consultation Draft* – cannot be justified on the basis that otherwise there would be significant negative implications for the South East's economy.

Affordable housing

- A somewhat higher level of housing growth in the South East could be justified on the grounds of meeting affordable housing needs. In the South East there are rising numbers of people living in temporary accommodation. The priority for the South East is to secure more affordable housing (both socially rented and intermediate) for those people already living within the region.

- There are reservations about the underlying methodology supporting the Barker Review's recommendations. It is unclear whether it is possible for policy makers to set targets for output in the housing market to achieve a particular path for house price inflation. The Barker Review came up with a national headline figure for an extra 141,000 dwellings per year to reduce real house price inflation to 1.1 per cent per annum. But research commissioned by ippr suggested that if only about half that figure were built nationally it would have a similar effect on house price inflation. This raises question marks over the robustness of the Barker methodology and the extent to which it can be relied upon to develop both national and regional affordability targets.

- To tackle affordability problems in the South East a direct increase in the provision of affordable housing would seem to be the most appropriate policy response. A range of different providers could deliver the extra affordable housing required.

Mixed communities and regeneration

- It is important to get the right mix between private sector housebuilding and the provision of various types of affordable housing to help create sustainable communities. This will not be achieved with levels of housebuilding lower than those proposed in the *South East Plan: Consultation Draft*. Levels of housebuilding above those options in the *South East Plan: Consultation Draft* would not be politically acceptable within the region.

- Simply building new housing in less prosperous areas will not per se deliver regeneration. The South East needs to take an approach to local regeneration that considers housing, transport and employment policies in an integrated way.

Developing incentives for sustainable choices

- If the South East is to maintain its current rate of economic growth, and offer its citizens a high quality of life, it will need to develop policy measures that influence the attitudes and behaviour of individuals and firms.

Traffic management and car dependency

- Despite residents in the South East citing increases in traffic congestion and pollution as two of their top local priorities, there are no signs of these quality of life pressures abating. By 2010, road traffic is expected to grow by 25 per cent in the South East, in part due to falling motoring costs but also because of deficiencies in public transport.

- The UK and congested regions like the South East are facing a tough choice between increasing traffic delays and pollution, or bold measures for managing traffic growth and improving public transport options. The success of the Central London congestion charge has helped build political momentum for the use of price signals in influencing travel behaviour. Maintaining this momentum will require significant upfront investment in transport infrastructure and strong political leadership before a national congestion charging scheme can be introduced.

- Over the longer term the South East should encourage the Government to press ahead with plans to introduce a national congestion charging scheme within the next ten years. There are also short to medium term pathways for cutting congestion such as local urban charging schemes and motorway tolling.

- It is up to local communities and not central government to decide whether an urban charging scheme is the best way to manage traffic demand in a local area. If the Government wants to see local urban charging being progressed in the South East and elsewhere, it will need to provide local authorities with funding for packages of measures that combine road pricing with local public transport improvements.

- The South East should explore options for introducing motorway tolling on congested commuter routes, as well as tolling on major motorway sections that are due to be widened, to help ease congestion on busy commuter routes. Motorway tolling schemes could be introduced as public-private partnerships whereby the financial risks, administration and revenue are shared with the private sector.

- Smarter travel measures, such as travel plans and public transport marketing, could also help to cut congestion whilst encouraging public transport use, cycling or walking in the South East and across the UK.

Water efficiency

- Only with significant water efficiency savings in existing and new homes, and the timely provision of new water resources, will there potentially be enough water to meet rising demand for new housing and domestic consumption in the region.

- Water metering and smarter tariffs can help to change people's attitudes to water use and encourage them to save water and money by using water efficient appliances and measures in their homes. Higher levels of water metering should be encouraged in areas of low water availability in the South East.

- There should be tougher regulations placed on developers to improve the water efficiency of new buildings. The voluntary Code for Sustainable Buildings should promote resource efficient buildings that use less water and energy and create less waste.

■ Water companies also have a greater role to play in reducing water leakage and encouraging greater water efficiency in both new and existing homes. The Government should introduce a water industry equivalent to the Energy Efficiency Commitment. Each water company could be set water efficiency targets for reducing levels of water consumption in both households and businesses. There should be a pilot of the Water Efficiency Commitment in the South East.

Meeting infrastructure needs

Resources for infrastructure

■ The UK needs an open debate about whether, as a nation, we are prepared to devote the resources necessary to deliver a range of housing policy objectives including the Government's Sustainable Communities Plan, and to meet other associated demands for improved infrastructure in areas such as transport.

■ There has been a legacy of under-spending on housing and transport in the UK. Both housing and transport saw sharp declines in public spending as a proportion of Gross Domestic Product (GDP) from the early 1990s.

■ The Government has dedicated extra public resources to delivering its sustainable communities agenda. The 2004 Spending Review included a commitment to fund an extra 10,000 social homes a year by 2008 (a 50 per cent increase in provision), and established a £200 million Community Infrastructure Fund for transport investment. To put this in perspective, £200 million was little more than one per cent of the public sector spend on transport in 2004-05.

■ The Government may be counting too much on other sources of funding. It is not clear that significant new affordable housing will be delivered through Section 106 agreements without public subsidy. While there may be the opportunity to use a land value tax in the future to capture value uplifts and help fund infrastructure improvements, this is a number of years away. The Government, however, needs to give priority to the development of land value taxation.

Infrastructure needs

■ It is clear that the Community Infrastructure Fund, as currently resourced, will be insufficient to meet the future additional transport infrastructure costs associated with the growth areas, particularly given the housing growth proposals in the Sustainable Communities Plan look out to 2016 and 2031.

■ In terms of protection from flooding, the Government is already committed to a relatively generous settlement of £564 million per year on coastal and flood defences in England and Wales over the period to 2007-08. Developers are also expected to make a contribution to the cost of new flood defences where they are needed to protect new buildings.

■ Of the new development planned for the South East growth areas, 30 per cent of the sites have been allocated in flood zone areas. However, the majority of these sites will be in areas where the annual probability of flooding is either low or moderate. Across all the growth areas, flood management measures will need to be periodically reviewed to ensure a high standard of protection.

■ The costs of providing new water and sewerage infrastructure will be largely borne by individual customers through their water bills. Some additional water and sewerage costs associated with new housing developments in the South East were considered in the 2005-10 Water Price Review period. It is unclear, however, if that provided for is sufficient to maintain security of water supply and water quality. Water resources are already stretched in the South East and so one-off investments may be required in the short to medium term for large-scale assets such as reservoirs, which would increase water bills.

Revenue from congestion charging

■ It is already the case that the people of the South East have become more and more dependent on their cars. This is in part because the costs of motoring have been falling, but also because there has been inadequate investment in public transport alternatives.

■ The principal purpose of congestion charging is to reduce journey times and traffic jams in some of the busiest hot spots. However, congestion charging could also potentially raise extra resources to pay for future transport improvements.

■ If politicians are to win public support for national congestion charging, in the years preceding the introduction of the scheme there will need to be increased public spending on transport to offer accessible, reliable and cost-effective transport options. But this presents a funding conundrum – whilst a national congestion charging scheme could potentially raise additional revenue to pay for transport improvements it will not do so for at least another decade. Bearing in mind public spending on transport will be limited over the next parliamentary term, the Government is faced with the problem of how it can start to invest in transport improvements over the short to medium term to make the longer term introduction of a national congestion charging scheme publicly palatable.

■ There needs to be a national political consensus for giving greater priority to transport investment. One option is to increase transport investment by financing it through extra government borrowing. This would not have consequences for the Treasury's 'golden rule' which allows for borrowing to finance investment. It would, however, increase the debt-GDP ratio and therefore the future burden of interest payments to be borne by the taxpayer. These interest payments could be met by some of the future revenues raised from a national congestion charging scheme.

■ Some of the future revenue raised from motorists should be redistributed back to the regions. But there is a trade-off between using the revenue gains from a national congestion charging scheme to fund upfront transport investment initially financed through borrowing, and using the revenue to pay for transport improvements in future decades. There will therefore need to be a balance between the two.

Spending priorities

■ The 2004 Spending Review implied that after 2005-06, the overall rate of growth in public spending will decline significantly, with spending as a proportion of GDP reaching a plateau of about 42 per cent. Spending on health, education and international development will rise as a proportion of GDP, which of course implies that the share of some other areas of public spending will need to fall.

■ The Commission's work suggests that policy makers may have got some of their priorities wrong and that the relative neglect of housing and transport could undermine the delivery of the Government's Sustainable Communities Plan. It could also make it less likely that key policy challenges such as the introduction of a national congestion charging scheme will secure the necessary popular support. It may be time for a rethink of some of the Government's future spending priorities.

Improving governance and planning arrangements

■ There is a plethora of overlapping authorities and agencies in the South East responsible for housing, planning, and transport policy and delivery. There is a need for better co-ordination both within the South East and across the Greater South East.

Governance arrangements

■ To help join up strategic policy-making at the regional level the Government should create a single Housing, Planning and Transport Regional Board for advising ministers on strategic spending priorities across policy areas as well as the possibility of switching funding between them. The Board should support democratic accountability by being made up of elected local authority representatives from the Regional Assembly alongside senior representatives from business, the environmental and voluntary sectors, and relevant agencies. It should promote subsidiarity by not eroding the powers of local authorities.

■ To reflect the strong rail linkages between London, the South East and East of England, the Government should create a Greater South East Rail Authority with responsibility for the franchising of rail passenger services across the Greater South East (excluding inter-city rail journeys).

■ A Greater South East Housing Forum should be established for providing strategic oversight of inter-regional housing issues across London, the South East and East of England.

Flexible planning

■ The South East Plan is due to set the policy framework for housing between 2006 and 2026. But given the limitations in housing data, including uncertainty over future international migration patterns, setting housebuilding targets for 20 years hence does not seem sensible. Shorter planning horizons may be more appropriate, enabling more flexible and strategic responses to housing needs in the South East.

Locally sensitive planning

- Across the South East, there needs to be a locally sensitive approach to planning and delivering new development which requires strong leadership by local authorities. As elected bodies, local authorities have a legitimacy that can allow them to deal with contentious issues in a way that enables greater public understanding and acceptance of those issues. It should be up to local authorities to identify the appropriate balance of affordable housing needs (the mix of socially rented and intermediate housing) within their communities. They should be responsive to changing needs over time and promote the development of mixed communities.

- Local authorities often complain that one of the biggest blocks to bringing forward new development is the lack of incentives. The funding of local infrastructure improvements alongside new developments is often seen a critical issue by residents. If new developments, particularly affordable housing, were prioritised for local infrastructure funding this could provide local authorities with the incentive they need to win public support for new developments.

Water, flooding and planning

- There should be greater integration of issues relating to the availability of water resources, water quality and flood risk into local and regional development processes. In some cases, concerns about water scarcity, water quality and/or flood risk may be grounds for refusal of planning permission.

- There needs to be greater clarity over the co-ordination of, and responsibility for sewerage and drainage issues, especially as the incidence of urban flooding is likely to increase over the coming decades.

- Planning guidance directing development away from locations with a high flood risk needs to be enforced more rigorously. The Environment Agency could be made a statutory consultee for all new developments in flood risk locations. As a last resort the Government may have to intervene to ensure that no inappropriate development takes place in flood zone areas.

Conclusions

If the South East is to maintain its economic success while enhancing the environment and improving the wellbeing and quality of life of all its citizens, it will need to develop a new approach to growth and consumption. The focus for policy should be on achieving a sustainable rate of growth in output per head and disposable household income, rather than just maximising the growth in GDP. Policy-makers in the South East and in government need to develop measures that influence the behaviour of individuals and firms to enable and encourage the more efficient use of natural resources that results in less pollution and waste. There will need to be investments in infrastructure, particularly public transport improvements for helping to reduce car dependency.

If the South East is to improve the wellbeing of all its citizens, reducing economic disparities within the region and improving the availability of affordable housing will be essential. The key to reducing disparities will be to raise employment rates in less prosperous parts of the South East and among disadvantaged groups. There will need to be additional public funding for meeting affordable housing needs.

From the point of view of the South East, boosting the economic performance of the less prosperous regions in the UK would make it easier for the region to cope with the problems that current levels of relative economic prosperity pose. This would help to ease the pressures on the region that have been generated by the relative shift in economic activity and population to the Greater South East. The Government should particularly focus on enhancing policies in relation to employment services and skills to raise employment rates in less prosperous regions.

An approach to growth, driven by quality of life priorities, that seeks to promote resource efficiency, reduce disparities within the region and support government efforts to address inter-regional disparities in economic performance, would be in the long term interest of the South East.

1. The problems of success: quality of life priorities in the South East

The Commission's goal is for the South East to maintain its economic success and its position as one of Europe's most prosperous regions, while at the same time enhancing its environment and improving the wellbeing and quality of life of all its citizens. The Commission shall take into account the position of the South East with regards to London as a world city and as the frontier to mainland Europe, as well as considering the UK's inter-regional disparities.

The South East is one of the most prosperous regions in the UK and in Europe. However, managing the problems posed by this relative success has become increasingly difficult. As a high growth region the South East already has high levels of car use and traffic pollution, as well as a lack of affordable housing. The impacts of climate change are likely to lead to more frequent water shortages during the summer months and more floods during the winter months.

The South East faces a fundamental choice. Either it carries on down the path of traditional economic growth, with higher levels of congestion, worsening air quality and greater pressures on the natural environment. Or it chooses a sustainable future and takes the path of smarter growth – maintaining its economic prosperity but spreading the benefits to all its citizens, protecting the environment and safeguarding the region for future generations. Part of this will involve focusing policy efforts on increasing employment rates within the region, especially in less prosperous areas and among disadvantaged groups. It will also require policy measures for encouraging and enabling individuals and firms to consume resources more efficiently and produce less waste and pollution. Ultimately, the South East needs to develop a new approach to growth, driven by quality of life priorities, that ensures a sustainable future.

On the whole, people in the South East rate their quality of life highly. Surveys of public attitudes to quality of life reveal that there are a wide range of issues that people say they care about which cover almost every area of public policy. However, the key problems and issues that people express concerns about in the South East relate to affordable housing and traffic congestion.

The Commission's work is focused on the South East as defined by the Government Office Region comprising seven county councils – Buckinghamshire, Hampshire, Kent, Oxfordshire, Surrey, East Sussex and West Sussex. The Commission is primarily interested in the natural resource use, social and environmental problems that tend to emerge from the pursuit of environmentally 'unsustainable' growth. The Commission's work has focused on issues relating to the economic performance of the South East; affordable housing needs; sustainable transport; water resources and flooding. The Commission has considered these issues, where possible, within the context of the South East's inter-relationship with London, the rest of the UK and Europe.

Widening how we think about quality of life

For years, many observers have argued that Gross Domestic Product (GDP), as a measure of economic output, is an inadequate yardstick for quality of life. The economist Richard Easterlin highlighted the limitations of using GDP as a measure of wellbeing in his 1974 essay *Does Economic Growth Improve the Human Lot?* Yet the approach of successive governments has been to focus on maximising GDP growth as a principal, if not indeed overriding, policy objective. It has become apparent to policy-makers, both in the South East and in central government, that they need to widen how they measure success so that they are not solely reliant on economic indicators of performance, important though these are.

The issues that matter in the South East

Quality of life priorities

Most people in the South East say that they experience a high quality of life. Figure 1 shows that a recent MORI survey undertaken for the South East England Regional Assembly (SEERA) reported that 91 per cent of residents rated their quality of life as being either very good or fairly good. The most recent government survey found that attitudes towards quality of life were generally very positive across England with 83 per cent of people rating their quality of life as either very good or fairly good (Defra, 2002).

Figure 1: How people rate their quality of life in the South East, 2004

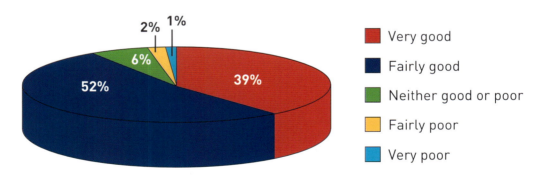

Source: MORI, 2004

However, asking people whether or not they are generally satisfied with their quality of life is not necessarily all that revealing. It is, perhaps, more useful to examine the survey evidence on what issues people thought were already posing, or could in future pose, a problem to their quality of life. This might give indications to policy-makers about the issues they need to address. Table 2 shows that people's top concerns in the South East relate to the cost and availability of housing, traffic levels and problems with public transport. ippr's analysis of Best Value Performance Indicators shows that concerns about affordable housing and traffic congestion were the top priorities in local areas throughout the South East – in both urban and rural areas and in both affluent and less prosperous parts of the region (Foley, 2004).

Table 1: For each of the following issues, which is a serious problem, a problem, or not a problem in the South East?

Problem	Serious problem	Problem	Not a problem	Don't know	Net
Cost of housing	66	19	7	8	86
Traffic levels	53	29	10	8	85
Housing shortage	34	24	26	15	58
Public transport	22	28	31	19	50
Lack of amenities	10	18	52	20	28
Job availability	8	20	50	22	28
Poor quality/lack of parks	5	16	62	17	21

Source: MORI, 2004

When the MORI survey asked people what concerns they had with building homes more quickly in the South East, 35 per cent were concerned that it would decrease the amount of open or green space available, 32 per cent were concerned that it would increase traffic, while 12 per cent were concerned that it would put pressure on water supply and sewerage systems (MORI, 2004).

Figure 2 shows how quality of life factors relating to transport, housing, pollution and access to green spaces varied across the English regions. Transport, housing and air pollution were of more concern in the Greater South East – London, the East of England and the South East – compared to the other English regions. These concerns appeared more acute in London than the South East. In this national survey, transport, housing and pollution were consistently rated as more important issues than access to green spaces, across the English regions including the South East.

Figure 2: The variation in quality of life factors across the English regions in 2001

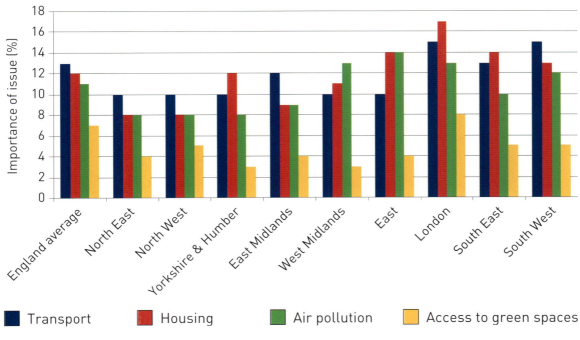

Source: Defra, 2002
Note: in this survey respondents were able to choose more than one issue of importance to them

Facing up to difficult choices

Political parties like to promote the concept of 'choice.' But every choice we make is conditioned and constrained by the choices others have already made, and this in turn conditions future choices (Levett et al., 2003). This can be illustrated using the example of car dependency, which is particularly relevant to the South East, which has high levels of car use and ownership (NTS, 2003). Car ownership can offer people the freedom to travel in a flexible way. But a high level of car use is adding to the congestion and pollution problems experienced by the population of the South East. This in turn is inhibiting the choices of others, as fewer people can now choose to cycle on roads that are not clogged up with cars, or live in areas free from traffic noise, where children can play safely in front of their homes.

Indeed, the choices that people make today have the potential to influence the choices available to people in the future. The fact that so many people in the South East choose to travel by car today is cumulatively adding to air pollution which will affect the health of their children by increasing their vulnerability to respiratory problems. This example highlights the classic conundrum facing policy-makers about how to balance the rights of the individual against the rights of wider society, as well as how to balance the rights of people today against the rights of people tomorrow.

It is important, however, not to create a false divide by pitting individual choices against the good of society. Ultimately, society is made up of individuals and all of us as individuals will have to manage the consequences of our choices. The choices of individuals in the South East will collectively contribute to the quality of life of the region, and there must be collective responsibility for finding the solutions for the benefit of current and future generations.

Inconsistencies in individual preferences

Most quality of life surveys are based on asking people about their individual preferences at a particular point in time. But there are often inconsistencies in people's preferences. For instance, most people in the South East recognise the need for new housing, yet at the same time are generally opposed to any new housing developments being built anywhere near where they live. Table 3 shows that half of the residents surveyed agreed that more housing was needed and about a third disagreed. But the proportions were reversed when people were asked about more homes in their local area, with only a third agreeing and about half disagreeing (MORI, 2004).

Table 2: To what extent do you agree or disagree that...

Problem	% disagree	% agree	% net agree
More homes are needed in the South East	32	50	+18
To tackle housing shortages, more homes need to be built more quickly in the South East	38	44	+6
More homes are needed in my local area	52	34	-18

Source: MORI, 2004

The survey revealed that people living in town centres, particularly in Oxfordshire, Buckinghamshire and Hampshire, were more likely to agree with the need for new housing in their local area compared to those living in rural areas, particularly in Kent and West Sussex. The results clearly illustrate that people are often reluctant to face up to difficult trade-offs when it comes to weighing up the advantages and disadvantages of new housing developments versus the quality of life impacts. The inconsistencies in people's preferences highlight the limitations on how far policy-makers can and should draw on quality of life survey evidence.

Future quality of life priorities in the South East

The famous Brundtland report for the 1987 World Commission on Environment and Development (WCED) proposed that sustainable developed should refer to: '...development that meets the needs of present generations without compromising the ability of future generations to meet their own needs' (WCED, 1987). Integral to most definitions of sustainability is the promotion of both inter-generational and intra-generational justice. In the South East, water shortages and flood risk present some shorter term pressures, but their effects will almost certainly intensify over future decades with climate change and increased development.

The South East is already referred to as a 'semi-arid' region with current levels of abstraction that are unsustainable. With the exception of London, the South East consumes more water per person than any other English region (Environment Agency, 2004). According to the UK Climate Impacts Programme, winters are likely to become wetter and summers warmer and drier across the UK, with the most dramatic changes in the South East. Climate change may well mean that droughts in the South East become more frequent (UKCIP, 2002).

The irony is that while the South East is facing water shortages, as a region it is also increasingly at risk from flooding. Over 235,000 existing properties in the South East have been identified as being at risk from flooding (Environment Agency, 2004). The South East faces some of the greatest development pressures outside of London. The Sustainable Communities Plan has targeted Milton Keynes and Ashford as growth areas (ODPM, 2003). Chapter 5 will examine the impact of future housing developments on water shortages and flood risk in the South East.

Quality of life surveys tend to provide a snapshot of people's current quality of life concerns but they rarely capture people's awareness of potential future risks, or problems they might not have yet experienced. The media attention given to recent high-profile flood events has highlighted the social and economic devastation that floods can have on communities. However, the insurance industry has expressed concerns that some people, especially the less affluent, still have a low awareness of flood risks (ABI, 2004).

The Government and other public agencies have a responsibility to raise public awareness of these future risks, so that people can make informed choices about the extent to which they are willing to accept them. It is unclear whether people would put more pressure on the Government and other public agencies to alter their approaches to development, if they had a better awareness of the impacts of flooding over the longer term. Alternatively, they might put pressure on the Government and other public agencies to improve flood warning mechanisms and to invest in developing engineering solutions for strengthening flood defences. When assessing quality of life priorities in the South East and elsewhere, it is important to consider both current and future quality of life priorities.

Economic growth, population growth and quality of life

ippr commissioned some modelling to help understand the environmental effects of different rates of economic growth and population growth in the South East (Foley, 2004). Under all the future economic growth and population growth scenarios explored, traffic levels, water usage and air emissions would continue to rise. The modelling illustrated that, even if policy-makers were to pursue a lower rate of economic growth and population growth in the South East, traffic levels, water usage and air emissions would continue to rise, albeit at a slower rate. Slowing the rate of economic growth and population growth in the South East will therefore not be sufficient to address the environmental problems and resource shortages facing the South East. What is needed are policy measures for influencing the behaviour of individuals and firms.

Influencing the behaviour of individuals and firms

This clearly highlights that if the South East is to maintain a reasonable rate of economic growth and offer its citizens a high quality of life it will need to develop policy measures that change the attitudes and behaviour of individuals and firms. This is a central message in the Government's Sustainable Development Strategy which focuses on the importance of 'getting more from less', by encouraging individuals and firms to adopt more sustainable consumption patterns in order to improve quality of life (Defra, 2005). The kinds of policy options that could be employed for delivering more sustainable consumption can be considered under four headings:

- **Information** – raising awareness of more sustainable products and services. For example, labelling household appliances so that consumers can make informed choices about the products they are using.

- **Incentives** – using price signals to influence people's behaviour and/or rewarding individuals who use resources efficiently. For example, tax breaks for resource efficient technologies, road user charging, or water metering.

- **Regulation** – requiring products or buildings to meet minimum efficiency standards. For example, regulations that require firms to develop and provide more resource efficient products or buildings.

- **Infrastructure** – supporting the provision of infrastructure and services that make it easier for people to change their consumption of products or use of services. For example, support for accessible and reliable public transport alternatives to the car such as more frequent local bus services.

The Government, agencies, authorities, firms and individuals in the South East need to take collective responsibility for improving quality of life in the region. Policy-makers need to identify policy options that encourage and enable individuals and firms to consume resources more efficiently, and produce less waste and pollution. Support for cleaner, more efficient technologies could also play an important role in promoting greater resource efficiency. For some of these options, authorities and agencies in the South East may have limited powers to influence the behaviour of individuals and firms in their region. Central government will therefore need to play an important role in funding infrastructure projects that support sustainable mobility and in developing fiscal incentives and regulations that promote resource efficiency.

As discussed in chapter 2, the South East is already, and is likely to remain, one of Europe's most prosperous regions. The challenge is to marry this relative economic success with enhancing the environment and improving the wellbeing and quality of life of all the region's citizens. Subsequent chapters look at the policy issues in housing, transport, and water and flooding that will need to be addressed if this challenge is to be met.

2. A successful region: the South East's economic performance

The South East is one of the most prosperous regions in the UK and in the European Union (EU). Of the UK's regions only London has a higher level of income per head. The South East is one of three regions with the highest levels of employment among its working age population. The economic performance of the South East compares well with what are generally regarded as the EU's most prosperous substantive regions containing all the well known centres of commerce in Europe outside of London and Paris.

However, there are serious disparities in economic prosperity within the South East, with certain groups (for example, people with disabilities) and certain areas (for example, Thanet) within the region continuing to have relatively low levels of employment. Tackling these disparities within the region should be a priority and would the best means of improving the region's overall economic performance.

Boosting the economic performance of the less prosperous regions in the UK would ease the pressures on the South East that have been generated by the relative shift in economic activity and population to the Greater South East. This in turn would make it easier for the region to cope with the problems that current levels of relative economic success pose, particularly in terms of traffic congestion, the lack of affordable housing, the use of natural resources and the quality of the environment.

This chapter looks at the relative economic performance of the South East, comparing it to the other regions of the UK and the EU. It examines disparities in economic performance within the region, highlighting differences in employment rates. It then discusses what the objectives should be for economic policy in the South East, placing emphasis on the employment agenda, before drawing together some key policy conclusions.

The South East's economic performance

Figure 1 shows that in 2003 the South East was responsible for about 16 per cent of the overall output (or Gross Value Added[1] (GVA)) of the UK economy, when the output of commuters is assigned to where they live (a residence based measure). The South East's economy is slightly smaller than London's on this measure. About 11 per cent of those in employment who live in the South East commute to work in London, which is one indication of the close economic relationship between the region and the capital city.

---

1   Gross Value Added (GVA) differs from Gross Domestic Product (GDP) in that GDP is measured at market prices, that is it is GVA plus taxes/less subsidies on products. Information on taxes and subsidies is, however, not available at a regional level.

Figure 1: Share of UK GVA by region (per cent), residence based, 2003

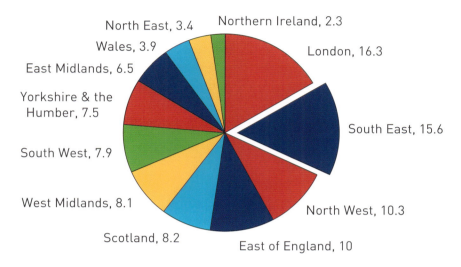

Source: ONS, 2004a

A plausible assumption is that about 85 per cent of the expenditure of London commuters takes place in the region in which they live (OEF, 2004). Thus, assigning the economic contribution of commuters to their region of residence is likely to give a more meaningful measure of the wellbeing and welfare of people, which is ultimately what we are concerned with. Of course the welfare or wellbeing of individuals and households will be related to the level of output *per head*, in other words adjusting for the size of the population in the region. Figure 2 shows that in 2003, output (or GVA) per head in the South East was about 15 per cent above the UK average (on a residence based measure).

Figure 2: GVA per head by region, residence based, 2003

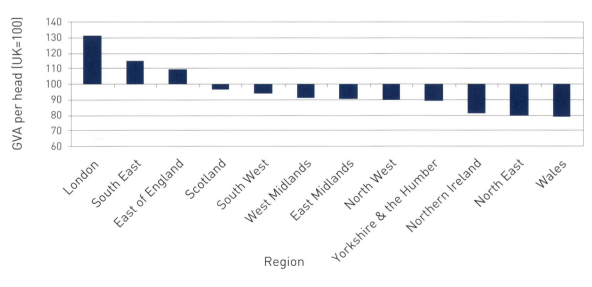

Source: ONS, 2004a

Aside from already being one of the UK's most prosperous regions, the South East appears to be the only UK region with a trend growth rate significantly above the UK or England average. Although there is no agreed methodology for measuring the trend growth rate of output per head, one set of plausible estimates from a consultancy is set out in Table 1. The North East and Wales are the two UK regions with a below average growth rate. Overall, the Government itself recognises that regional disparities in growth in the UK are significant and increasing (ODPM/ONS, 2005).

Table 1: Trend real growth rates, GVA per head, 1989-2000, per cent p.a.

Region	% Growth
South East	2.75
West Midlands	2.25
London	2.00
East of England	2.00
North West	2.00
Scotland	2.00
Northern Ireland	2.00
East Midlands	2.00
Yorkshire & the Humber	1.75
South West	1.75
Wales	1.50
North East	1.25

Note: Differences of one quarter of one percentage point from the UK/England average of two per cent should not be regarded as significant.
Source: EBS, 2004

There is clearly a very close economic relationship between the South East region and the world city it is next door to. About six per cent of the economic output of London is produced by commuters from the South East; 11 per cent of those in employment who live in the South East commute to work in London. It is pointless to debate whether it is the labour of the South East that helps drive the London economy or the buoyancy of the London economy that provides jobs for some of those that live in the South East. In economic and labour market terms there is no difference between someone who works in central London and happens to live in the London Borough of Sutton and someone who works in London and lives over the administrative boundary in Surrey.

Some observers have gone further than this to argue that London and much of the South East and East of England regions, and indeed parts of the South West region along the M4 corridor and the southern part of the East Midlands, constitute what is effectively one economic and labour market region for which policies need to be developed in an integrated way (LSE/Corporation of London, 2003). This 'super-region' might stretch from Swindon in the west to Cambridge and Northamptonshire in the north. Other attempts to measure London's Functional Urban Region, that is the region that has very strong linkages in economic and labour market terms, would certainly encompass parts of the South East reaching out to Maidstone and Crawley in the south and Guildford and Reading in the west (GLA Economics, 2004).

We have no inter-regional trade or regional input/output data for the UK economy that would allow us to trace precisely the pattern of linkages between the different regional economies. That is why it is best to be circumspect in claiming that any particular region drives the UK economy, or indeed acts as a black hole sucking vitality from the disadvantaged regions, which is the other story sometimes told. It is more sensible instead to emphasise the inter-dependence of the different regions of the UK.

Another very useful measure for comparing economic prosperity across and within regions is gross disposable household income per head. This is by definition a much more direct measure of the welfare or wellbeing of households. It includes the income derived from current economic activity, but also the income from past economic activity in the form of pension payments. Areas with a large pensioner population will compare less well on a measure of output (GVA) per head than on a measure of disposable household income per head. The latter also includes the redistributive impact of the tax and benefits system, one reason why the differences on this measure across the regions are significantly smaller than when using output (GVA) per head.

Importantly for the South East, the measure of gross disposable household income reported in Figure 3 does take into account interest payments on home loans. So it makes some adjustment for one of the biggest differences in the cost of living between the regions, relating to the costs of homeownership. Historically, one of the key problems with this and much other data has been our relative lack of knowledge about the differences in price levels between regions and the differences in inflation rates.

Figure 3 : Gross disposable household income per head, by region, 2003

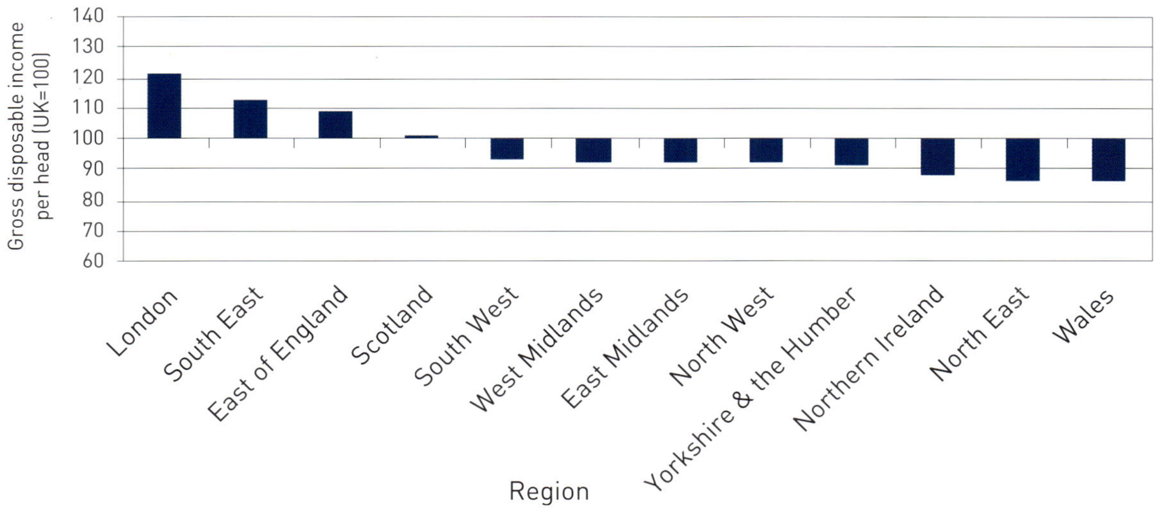

Source: ONS, 2005

However, even bearing this in mind, it is clear that disposable household income per head in the South East was significantly above the UK average in 2003 – about ten per cent above average. This is one of the key reasons why locating in the region would be so attractive for businesses – if real incomes were lower, as suggested by some (for example, SEEDA, 2005a), the region would not offer such a high level of demand for the goods and services produced by those businesses, who would have an incentive, therefore, to locate elsewhere.

The South East is one of the EU's most prosperous regions. Table 2 sets out the economic performance in 2001-2 of the 'regions' of the 15 states that made up the EU before the recent enlargement. Critically for these international comparisons, the EU's statistical agency, Eurostat, only collects data on output (or GDP/GVA) per head on a workplace based measure, where the contribution of commuters is assigned to where they work. So any comparisons using this data will understate the economic performance of any region which is next to a major city and sends a part of its workforce to work in that city, including of course the South East. For this reason, three of the 15 UK regions are entered twice in Table 2 – for the South East, London and the East of England, we have both the measure of output (GDP/GVA) per head on a workplace basis as reported by Eurostat, and the residence based measure converted by ippr from national data into a measure of output per head relative to the EU-15 average.

Table 2: The South East's economic performance compared with other EU regions

Region NUTS level 1	GDP/Head (PPS) 2001, EU15 = 100	GDP growth GDP growth, annual % change (1995-2001)	Employment rate % of population aged 15-64 (2002)	Population 1000 inhabitants (2001)
Regions significantly above the South East				
Reg. Bruxelles-Cap (BE)	217	2.6	54.5	971
Luxembourg (LU)	194	6.1	63.6	442
Hamburg (DE)	171	1.8	64.9	1,721
London (UK)	**165**	**4.6**	**68.7**	**7,188**
Île de France (FR)	165	2.8	66.4	11,055
London (UK)	142	4.6	68.7	7,188
Bremen (DE)	136	1.5	60.7	660
Regions not significantly different from the South East				
Lombardia (IT)	131	1.9	63.2	9,150
Emilia-Romagna (IT)	126	1.9	67.5	4,023
South East (UK)	126	4.1	77.0	8,007
West-Nederland (NL)	126	3.4	74.9	7,473
Hessen (DE)	124	2.0	67.5	6,073
Ostösterreich (AT)	119	2.2	68.4	3,395
Ireland (IE)	118	9.2	65.0	3,853
Nord Est (IT)	118	1.9	63.4	6,692
Bayern (DE)	117	2.5	70.7	12,280
Eastern (UK)	116	3.3	76.1	5,395
South East (UK)	**116**	**4.1**	**77.0**	**8,007**
Danmark (DK)	115	2.5	75.9	5,357
Baden-Württemberg (DE)	114	2.2	69.9	10,561
Nord Ovest (IT)	113	1.5	61.1	6,030
Westösterreich (AT)	113	2.6	70.6	2,893
Comunidad de Madrid (ES)	112	4.2	62.8	5,218
Lazio (IT)	111	1.8	55.0	5,322
Regions significantly below the South East				
Zuid-Nederland (NL)	107	3.3	74.4	3,525
Centro (IT)	107	2.2	61.5	5,870
Sverige (SV)	106	2.9	73.6	8,896
Noord-Nederland (NL)	106	2.8	72.1	1,678
Vlaams Gewest (BE)	106	2.5	63.5	5,960
Finland (FI)	104	4.1	68.1	5,188
Centre-Est (FR)	103	2.8	64.8	7,055
Nordrhein-Westfalen (DE)	102	1.2	63.2	18,027
Eastern (UK)	**101**	**3.3**	**76.1**	**5,395**
Noreste (ES)	101	3.6	61.8	4,044

Scotland (UK)	**100**	**1.5**	**70.3**	**5,064**
East Midlands (UK)	**97**	**2.5**	**73.5**	**4,175**
Südösterreich (AT)	96	2.6	67.5	1,744
Oost-Nederland (NL)	96	3.2	74.5	3,367
West Midlands (UK)	**95**	**2.3**	**71.2**	**5,267**
North West (UK)	**95**	**2.6**	**69.4**	**6,732**
Est (FR)	94	1.8	64.8	5,202
Este (ES)	94	3.7	63.3	11,123
South West (UK)	**94**	**2.7**	**76.2**	**4,934**
Saarland (DE)	93	0.8	61.9	1,067
Bassin Parisien (FR)	92	1.9	63.2	10,486
Sud-Ouest (FR)	92	2.8	62.9	6,267
Schleswig-Holstein (DE)	92	1.3	65.8	2,796
Yorkshire & the Humber (UK)	**91**	**2.1**	**70.5**	**4,967**
Niedersachsen (DE)	91	1.6	64.6	7,940
Ouest (FR)	91	3.0	64.9	7,884
Rheinland-Pfalz (DE)	90	1.3	67.0	4,041
Méditerranée (FR)	90	2.9	56.5	7,226
Berlin (DE)	90	-1.0	60.1	3,386
Nord Pas-de-Calais (FR)	83	2.2	54.1	4,014
Wales (UK)	**83**	**1.8**	**66.3**	**2,903**
Abruzzo-Molise (IT)	83	1.7	54.8	1,609
Northern Ireland (UK)	**82**	**2.7**	**64.8**	**1,689**
North East (UK)	**80**	**0.8**	**65.6**	**2,517**
Canarias (ES)	79	4.8	57.6	1,737
Madeira (PT)	78	5.0	65.1	244
Région Wallonne (BE)	77	1.9	54.8	3,351
Sardegna (IT)	76	2.2	46.7	1,646
Attiki (GR)	71	3.4	57.0	3,904
Continente (PT)	71	3.5	68.5	9,811
Noroeste (ES)	70	2.9	55.7	4,307
Centro (ES)	69	2.8	56.1	5,265
Sachsen (DE)	67	1.0	61.0	4,405
Brandenburg (DE)	67	2.2	61.9	2,597
Thüringen (DE)	66	2.1	62.5	2,421
Kentriki Ellada (GR)	66	3.2	57.7	2,425
Mecklenburg-Vorpommern (DE)	66	1.2	58.9	1,768
Sachsen-Anhalt (DE)	65	1.6	59.5	2,598
Sicilia (IT)	65	2.1	41.9	5,071
Campania (IT)	65	2.3	41.9	5,783
Sud (IT)	65	2.0	44.4	6,731
Sur (ES)	64	4.0	50.7	8,573
Voreia Ellada (GR)	63	3.8	55.2	3,516
Départements d'Outre-Mer (FR)	58	3.5	44.3	1,724
Açores (PT)	56	3.9	61.5	238

Note: GDP per head is workplace based except for the second entries, in red, for London, the South East and the Eastern region, which are residence based.

Source: Eurostat/EC, 2004

Because these estimates of output (GDP/GVA) per head are just that – estimates subject to some margin of error – Table 2 should not be read as a league table, as one cannot treat as significant small differences between regions. Instead, it separates out the regions into three groups: those regions where output per head is significantly above levels in the South East; those regions where it is not significantly different; and those regions where output per head is significantly lower. Table 2 also has data on the average annual GDP growth in the EU regions over the period 1995-2001 and the employment rate, expressed as a proportion of the working age population (15-64) in employment. It also has the populations of the regions, based on the intuition that it only makes sense to compare regions with broadly similar populations rather than, say, Bayern (Bavaria) and Luxembourg.

Only six EU regions in 2001-2 had levels of output (GDP/GVA) per head significantly higher than the South East. One of these is London; another is the French region containing Paris; the cities of Brussels, Hamburg and Bremen and the country of Luxembourg are the others. It does not, however, seem right to compare the South East region with any of these major cities, and certainly not the world cities of London and Paris.

Around 15 EU regions in 2001-02 had levels of output (GDP/GVA) per head similar to the South East. These include the nations of Ireland and Denmark; the region containing Spain's capital city; the region containing Italy's capital, the northern Italian regions that contain the cities of Milan, Turin, Bologna and Venice; the German regions that include the cities of Frankfurt, Munich and Stuttgart; the Dutch region that includes Amsterdam, and the Austrian regions that include Vienna and Salzburg. A comparison with the South East's output per head measured on a residence basis, taking into account the contribution of commuters to London, may be the fairest. Most of these regions have substantial populations that are broadly comparable with the South East. One should be cautious in making comparisons between the South East and other small countries and with regions that include their country's capital city. Only Ireland has had a faster GDP growth rate over the period 1995-2001 and Madrid has grown at a similar rate. Denmark and the Dutch region containing Amsterdam have rates of employment approaching those in the South East. All the other 54 EU regions in 2001-02 had levels of output (GDP/GVA) per head significantly below the South East.

The South East compares well with what are generally regarded as the EU's most prosperous substantive regions containing all the well known centres of commerce in Europe outside of London and Paris. This conclusion is a very positive one for the South East.

Disparities within the South East

The South East is not uniformly prosperous. There are important intra-regional economic disparities, but, as with international comparisons, it is important to consider the appropriateness of using different data to map out those disparities, especially when the data is arranged by administrative boundaries. Table 3 shows output (GVA) per head (on a workplace based measure), gross disposable household income per head and the employment rate for the sub-regions (or NUTS level 2 regions), and counties and cities (NUTS level 3) that make up the South East.

Table 3: Measures of economic prosperity at the sub-regional level

Region (NUTS levels 2 and 3)	GVA per head (UK=100) workplace based, 2002	Gross disposable income per head (UK=100), 2002	Employment rate, 2002 (%16-59/64)
Berkshire, Buckinghamshire and Oxfordshire	141	118	
Berkshire	165	117	80.4
Milton Keynes	145	97	82.2
Buckinghamshire CC	119	133	78.3
Oxfordshire	124	115	84.0
Surrey, East and West Sussex	111	123	
Brighton and Hove	97	106	76.8
East Sussex CC	70	108	76.6
Surrey	135	140	81.3
West Sussex	106	115	79.4
Hampshire and Isle of Wight	98	104	
Portsmouth	114	85	79.7
Southampton	110	84	75.1
Hampshire CC	97	112	81.9
Isle of Wight	62	91	73.8
Kent	81	102	
Medway	68	94	77.7
Kent CC	84	104	75.9

Note: The lower and upper confidence intervals for the employment rates range from plus or minus 1.5 to three percentage points. Thus the employment rate for the Isle of Wight is between 71.2 per cent and 76.5 per cent. NUTS refers to Nomenclature of Units for Territorial Statistics.

Source: ONS, 2004b; ONS, 2005; and ONS/LFS, 2004

According to the data on output per head, Portsmouth and Southampton are relatively prosperous and the Isle of Wight is the least prosperous part of the region. But the output per head of Portsmouth and Southampton will be biased upwards because they are cities drawing in commuters from beyond the city administrative boundaries. The Isle of Wight has a large retired population whose pension income will not be counted as part of current output (GVA) but will make up a significant part of household income. On this latter measure there is little to choose between the two cities and the Isle of Wight, if anything, households on the Isle of Wight have higher levels of disposable income. Indeed, with household income the city effect works in the other direction, because residence patterns and housing markets tend to work in a way that concentrates more of the less prosperous and lower income households in cities.

The employment data, analysed using administrative boundaries, tells a somewhat different story again, but then these boundaries do not constitute self-contained labour markets anyway. Figure 4, which maps employment rates for the travel-to-work areas that make up the South East region, probably gives the best indicator of the disparities in economic prosperity within the region. The relatively low employment rate for Thanet stands out – its employment rate is below 70 per cent, making it more comparable to the labour markets of the North East than the South East. One of the key challenges facing the region is dealing with these significant disparities in prosperity, with differential employment rates probably the best measure of the problem.

Figure 4: Employment rate by travel-to-work area, 2002

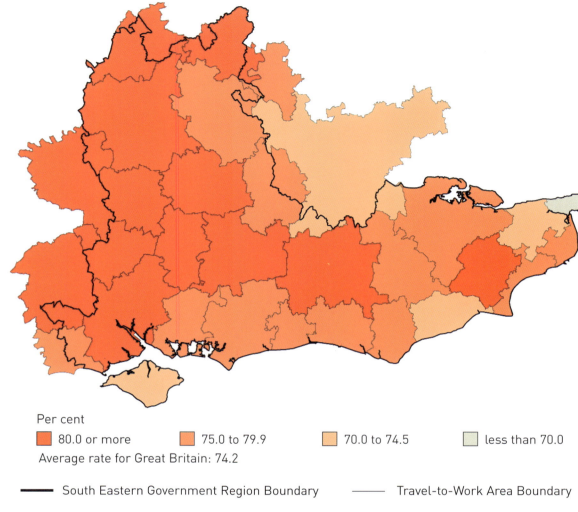

Per cent

■ 80.0 or more   ■ 75.0 to 79.9   ■ 70.0 to 74.5   ☐ less than 70.0

Average rate for Great Britain: 74.2

▬▬ South Eastern Government Region Boundary   ▬▬ Travel-to-Work Area Boundary

Note: The lower and upper confidence intervals for the employment rates range from plus or minus 1.5 to three percentage points. Thus the employment rate for the Isle of Wight is between 71.2 per cent and 76.5 per cent.

Source and ©: ONS, 2004c

The South East is one of three English regions that have employment rates approaching 80 per cent of the population aged from 16-59/64. It also has one of the lowest unemployment rates, at around four per cent of the workforce using the internationally agreed measure of unemployment.

It is, however, important not to overemphasise the tightness of the South East labour market. Table 4 reports the proportion of the adult population that was claiming a key benefit in the region in November 2004: 8.5 per cent of the adult population was claiming a key benefit and, of these, three-fifths were claiming benefits relating to sickness and disability. This figure is well below the national average, but gives some indication of the level of labour market exclusion that does still exist in the region.

Table 4: Claimants of key benefits by statistical group, November 2004

Claimant group	South East		Great Britain	
	% of population aged 16-59/64	Number of claimants (000s)	% of population aged 16-59/64	Number of claimants (000s)
Unemployed	1.3	65	2.1	739
Sick/disabled	5.5	271	8.6	3,070
Lone parents	1.5	75	2.1	763
Other	0.4	17	0.6	200
Total	8.6	429	13.3	4,771

Source: DWP/ONS, 2005

There is another piece of evidence to discuss on the state of the South East labour market. Table 5 is drawn from the National Employer Skills Survey (LSC, 2003) that is used in England to gauge the extent of unfilled vacancies, hard-to-fill vacancies, skill-shortage vacancies and skills gaps. This survey suggests that the South East has only modestly higher levels of unfilled vacancies and hard-to-fill vacancies when compared with the average for England, while the level of skill-shortage vacancies is the same. The incidence of reported skills gaps is also very close to the national average. Comparisons over time using this data are problematic, but there is no evidence that these constraints have been getting any worse, if anything they have been easing. This is not consistent with a portrait of an overly tight labour market, though the aggregate picture covers a much more complex story of recruitment problems for certain types of labour in certain sub-regional labour markets (Brooks, 2004). This survey evidence shows that the skill shortages that do exist are surprisingly evenly spread across both high and low skilled occupations.

Table 5: Incidence of vacancies, hard-to-fill and skill-shortage vacancies and skills gaps, 2001 & 2003 (per cent of total employment)

	South East		England	
	2001	2003	2001	2003
All vacancies	4.6	3.5	3.7	3.1
Hard-to-fill vacancies	2.5	1.5	1.7	1.2
Skill-shortage vacancies	1	0.6	0.8	0.6
Skills gaps	9.6	10	9.3	11

Source: National Employer Skills Survey, LSC, 2003

The labour market in the South East then is relatively tight but it is not overheating and there are still uncomfortable levels of labour market exclusion for some groups. Skill shortages and skills gaps do not seem to be a bigger problem in the South East than in other English regions and are not getting worse. Critically, the quantity and the quality of the labour force in the South East is not, at the moment, a serious constraint on growth in the region.

The objectives of economic policy in the South East

There is something of a paradox currently with regard to the objectives of public policy, in relation to the economic performance of the South East and the other English regions. At first sight, the goals of key agencies within the South East region appear to be out of line with government policy, because government policy is ostensibly aimed at increasing the rate of economic growth in the region, while the agencies either see the current rate as acceptable or indeed acknowledge that future rates of growth might be somewhat lower than those achieved recently. In fact, the real gap is that government policy is moving decisively towards emphasising increased *employment* as the key to improving economic performance in the regions, while key agencies in the South East downplay the importance of the employment agenda.

Currently, the primary objective of government policy for each English region, including the South East, is to increase the trend rate of growth of output per head. This objective is set out in the Government's Public Service Agreement (PSA) target relating to regional economic performance. This target was first announced in the 2000 Spending Review and the latest 2004 version is set out below.

> Make sustainable improvements in the economic performance of all English regions by 2008, and over the long-term reduce the persistent gap in growth rates between the regions, demonstrating progress by 2006 (joint between the ODPM, DTI and HM Treasury) (HMT, 2004).

The target has two components to it: first, to improve growth rates in all regions and, second, to reduce the gap in growth rates between the regions. The latter is not, however, a commitment to reducing absolute disparities in economic prosperity between the regions, even though, as Table 1 made clear and as the Government has recognised, those disparities seem to be widening further.

In straightforward accounting terms, the level of output (GVA/GDP) in an economy will be a function of the amount of labour that is being used in an economy and the efficiency with which that labour is being used. That is why the level of *employment* and the level of *productivity* are the other two main economic measures that are frequently reported, and are the subject of public policy designed to lead to their improvement. The employment rate is usually measured as the proportion of the working age population that is in paid employment. Productivity is best measured in terms of output per hour worked, but often output per person employed is used, especially in international comparisons, because of problems with measuring hours of work.

The most important 'killer fact' of the European economies is that GDP per head in the UK, Germany, France and Italy is very similar. Regional disparities in the UK, while serious, are similar in magnitude to disparities in Germany and France, but not as serious as in Italy (see Adams, Robinson and Vigor, 2003). This pattern is mirrored in the disbursement of EU structural funds: over the period 2000-06, the UK, France and Germany will receive a similar level of funding as a proportion of GDP, but Italy will receive twice as much.

Britain's level of GDP per head relative to its European partners is, in straightforward accounting terms, the result of a relatively high level of employment and a relatively lower level of productivity, measured in terms of output per hour worked. In Germany, France and Italy, it is the other way round: lower levels of employment but higher levels of productivity. This has led many UK policy-makers to argue for more priority to be given to improving the UK's productivity performance. However, the levels of employment and productivity in an economy are jointly determined by the structures and policy framework in place in that economy. For example, the tax structure or the structure of product and labour market regulation might favour more or less capital or labour intensive forms of economic activity in an economy. The Organisation for Economic Co-operation and Development (OECD) has observed an overall inverse relationship between productivity and employment among the most successful industrial economies (OECD, 2004). Overall, countries that have high levels of employment tend to have lower levels of productivity; high levels of productivity are associated with lower levels of employment. Public policy cannot proceed on the basis that you can hold employment constant and just concentrate on improving productivity. That is true for the UK as a whole, but is also true for a region like the South East where employment rates are particularly high.

The *South East Plan: Consultation Draft* published in January 2005 (SEERA, 2005) proposed the adoption of a target of three per cent growth per annum in output (GVA), which is line with the Regional Economic Strategy (SEEDA, 2002) and is supported by the South East England Development Agency (SEEDA). With the forecast increase in population, this would equate to an annual growth rate in output (GVA) per head of about 2.5 per cent. As the Plan recognised, this would be a somewhat lower rate of growth than that achieved in recent years. The *South East Plan: Consultation Draft* assumes a rate of growth in employment of about 0.7 per cent per annum over the period covered by the Plan, which is half the rate of growth over the period 1992-2002. Productivity growth is assumed to remain fairly steady. Meanwhile, the chair of SEEDA is quoted as saying that 'There is a broad consensus for continued economic growth in the region at current levels' (SEEDA, 2005b). What no-one in the region appears to be arguing for is an *increased* rate of growth in the South East, as would be required to meet the Government's current PSA target.

In the meantime, however, the thrust of government policy has been changing. Whether one looks at the 'five-year plans' of the DWP (2005) or the ODPM (2005), the emphasis is on the Government's long-term aspiration of increasing the employment rate in the UK to 80 per cent of all adults aged 15-64. This emphasis is consistent with the focus of the EU's Lisbon agenda on increasing employment rates across Europe (European Commission, 2005). In 2004, 73 per cent of working-age adults were in employment in the UK, which indicates the scale of ambition. The timescale for achieving an 80 per cent employment rate is not specified, but the way the target is framed gives a significant clue. Currently, the employment rate is measured as a proportion of the working age population defined as men aged 16-64 and women aged 16-59, reflecting the current state pension age, which is lower for women. However, it is to increase to 65 for women by 2020, so the new target relates to all adults up to this age. The expectation of the Government is that this change in the state pension age for women will result in a significant increase in employment among older women. Indeed, the Government explicitly links the two issues, recognising that more people staying in work for longer is the best solution to dealing with the problems facing the pensions system. All of these changes will, of course, occur within the time frame of the South East Plan which looks out to 2026.

In terms of dealing with regional economic disparities, the ODPM now puts the focus squarely on tackling high levels of economic inactivity among key groups, but especially those inactive due to sickness and disability. Because levels of economic inactivity are highest in the disadvantaged regions, including the North East and Wales, this agenda has an in-built 'bias' in favour of these regions: they simply have more to make up in terms of reducing economic inactivity. However, as we have seen, there are serious disparities in levels of employment within the South East and inactivity due to sickness and disability is an issue even in a region with a relatively tight labour market.

What has been somewhat de-emphasised in government policy is the productivity agenda. For a long period of time, much official analysis of regional disparities tried, rather unsuccessfully, to use the framework for analysing productivity differences between countries to understand the differences in economic performance between regions (for further discussion see Adams, Robinson and Vigor, 2003). For example, differences in private sector investment do seem to help explain some of the differences in productivity between countries, but they do not seem to explain any of the differences between the regions of the UK. Moreover, many of the key policies that are likely to impact on productivity are national policy tools, relating to competition policy, the tax and regulatory structure and fiscal support for investment, and science and innovation, a fact that regional agencies are well aware of. This is not to say that measures to improve productivity at a regional level are no longer seen as relevant, only that there has been a clear shift in emphasis towards the employment agenda.

However, agencies within the South East do not seem to have recognised this shift. Documents such as SEEDA's Corporate Plan continue to emphasise the 'five drivers of productivity' that had featured heavily in earlier government reports (SEEDA, 2005a). The *South East Plan: Consultation Draft* (SEERA, 2005) sounds a cautious note about achieving anything more than a modest increase in the employment rate in the region. But, even in a region where the overall employment rate is high, there is still plenty of scope for increasing employment.

To show why this is the case, we can return to the Government's target of an 80 per cent employment rate for all adults aged 16-64. The rate for the UK in 2004 on this measure was about 73 per cent. The employment rate in the South East on this measure was about 77 per cent (as can be seen in Table 2). The employment rate in the South East then is lower than the average rate the Government would like to achieve for the UK as a whole (by about 2020). As one of the UK's most economically successful regions, the South East would be expected to do better than the average. In the spirit of the objective of narrowing overall regional disparities, regions like the North East would be expected to achieve a much greater increase in their employment rate, but there is still likely to be some dispersion in employment rates around a national average of 80 per cent. One might hypothesise that the South East might be expected to boost its employment rate to around 82-83 per cent.

In 2004 about 4.1 million people were in employment in the region. At current levels of population, meeting the Government's target might imply an extra 300,000 or so people in employment from *within* the region. The region's population is, of course, expected to grow, but more of the region's requirement for an expanding workforce could be met from within the region, if employment rates in the region were raised.

The *South East Plan: Consultation Draft* sets out three different options for housing growth within the region (discussed in further detail in chapter 3). In its response to the Consultation Draft (SEEDA, 2005c) SEEDA argues that a housing growth rate of 32,000 per annum (the highest rate suggested in the Consultation Draft) could result in a labour shortfall in the region of 273,000 by 2026, as too few extra people could be accommodated in the region through in-migration. The estimated labour shortfall with a housing growth rate of 28,000 per year would be 339,000. However, if employment could be raised within the region by around 300,000 by meeting the Government's targets for raising the employment rate, these shortfalls would be more or less eliminated, without the need for higher levels of in-migration. There needs to be a balance between in-migration and mobilising the labour supply within the region, to meet future demand for both highly qualified and less skilled labour.

The work done by Deloitte for SEEDA confirms that determined action to raise employment rates within the region would significantly reduce any mooted labour shortfall (SEEDA, 2005c). A reduction in the number of economically inactive of about 265,000 over the lifetime of the Plan would mean that, at a housing growth rate of 32,000 per annum, the labour shortfall would be just 46,000 compared with overall growth of 805,000 in employment implied by the *South East Plan: Consultation Draft*. With a housing growth rate of 28,000 per annum, the labour shortfall would be 113,000. This would be the equivalent of reducing the rate of growth in employment from 0.7 per cent per annum to 0.6 per cent per annum and thus the overall growth rate in output from three per cent a year to 2.9 per cent a year. This is hardly the worrying decline in economic performance that has been suggested. Because the slight reduction in the rate of growth of employment and output, at a housing growth rate of 28,000 per annum, would be matched by a similar reduction in the rate of growth of the population, the growth in output per head would be little changed. It is the latter that is the ultimate measure of the relative economic prosperity of the region.

There is a range of policy instruments that might help in achieving the increase in employment within the region that is so important to maintaining its relative economic prosperity. We can quickly highlight one of the most important ways in which the extra labour force might be generated. In 2003-04, 39 per cent of women aged 59-64 were in employment in the South East, compared with 65 per cent of men in this age group. We should expect women's employment rates to begin to converge on men's employment rates for this age group, as has happened for other age groups over recent decades. We should also expect the employment rate for men in this age group to increase as government efforts to raise the effective retirement age make an impact. Overall employment rates may remain lower for women, in part because they are likely to continue to bear the burden of caring responsibilities (in the case of older women for sick or disabled spouses and older relatives, rather than children).

However, if the employment rate for women aged 59-64 in the South East increased to 70 per cent by about 2020 and the employment rate for men to 80 per cent, this would result in an additional 78,000 women and 37,000 men in work (based on the current population). The Government has explicitly emphasised the target of an extra 1 million older workers (over 50) in employment nationally (DWP, 2005). The South East's share of this might approach about 140,000, given its share of total employment in the UK. The DWP also has specific numbers in mind for the reduction in those claiming benefits relating to sickness and disability and as lone parents. Given the relative levels of inactivity in the South East reported in Table 4, these national targets would imply about 90,000 fewer people claiming benefits relating to sickness and disability and about 30,000 fewer lone parents claiming out-of-work benefits in the region.

The quality of jobs

It is of course important not only to consider overall levels of employment, but the quality of jobs on offer. The best way to do this is to look at the distribution of employment by occupation. Figure 5 shows the changes in the structure of employment by occupational group over the period from 1992 to 2002 and, for what they are worth, forecast changes out to 2012, which unsurprisingly show the same patterns of change continuing. The top three categories of the Standard Occupational Classification are designed to encompass those managerial, professional and technical jobs that demand high levels of qualifications, skills and/or experience and knowledge across all industrial sectors. In 2002, 44 per cent of the workforce in the South East worked in these occupations, up from 37 per cent in 1992 and compared with 40 per cent across the UK as a whole in 2002.

Figure 5: Occupational change in the South East, 1992-2012 (% of total employment)

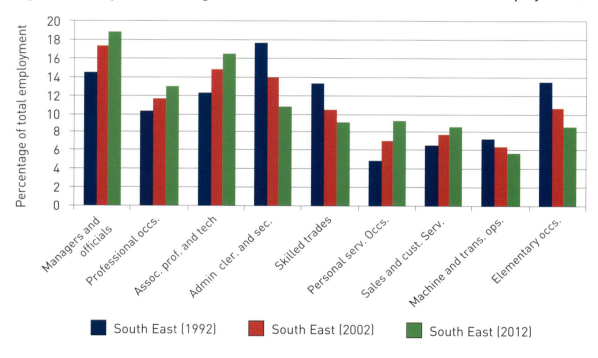

South East (1992)   South East (2002)   South East (2012)

Source: Working Futures Regional Report, University of Warwick, 2003-04

This occupational data has been used to make a broad distinction between 'good' and 'bad' jobs, though of course this involves making some strong value judgements. Managerial, professional and technical jobs are 'good' jobs, defined in terms of their relative pay as well as their demands for education and experience. Jobs in the personal service, and sales and customer service occupations might be defined as 'bad' jobs in terms of their relative pay. They have increased their share of total employment in the South East from 11.5 per cent to 15 per cent over the period 1992-2002. However, the elementary or unskilled manual occupations are also 'bad' jobs on the same basis and their share has declined from around 16 per cent to nearly 13 per cent over the same period, leaving the overall share of 'bad' jobs up by only one percentage point, compared with growth of seven percentage points in the proportion of 'good' jobs. The major declines in employment in the South East, as nationally, have occurred in the 'middle' of the labour market, among the administrative, clerical and secretarial occupations and the skilled trades, with their share of employment in the South East down from 31 per cent of the total in 1992 to 24 per cent in 2002. The 'middle' of the labour market has hollowed out to a certain extent, but these jobs have primarily been replaced by jobs at the 'top' end of the labour market.

The relatively high incidence of such jobs in the South East economy also helps explain why an above average proportion of the South East labour force holds higher qualifications at level four and above – about 30 per cent of the working age population in 2004 compared with 26 per cent for England as a whole. The South East has always been able to draw highly qualified labour from national and international markets. A much smaller proportion of the workforce in the South East has no qualifications – just ten per cent in 2004 compared with 13 per cent in England as a whole. The South East is also the region with the smallest proportion of its working-age population lacking basic skills, with 12 per cent having significant problems with their literacy in 2002-03 compared with 16 per cent in England as a whole (DfES, 2003). This still amounts to around 600,000 people in the region, though very few people believe that their lack of basic skills has had any impact on their ability to obtain work or perform their jobs.

Of course, policy-makers should be concerned about whether the skills and qualifications of those adults at risk of exclusion from the labour market may help, in part, to explain that exclusion, and should also pay attention to the attainment of young people in the education and training system. Policy-makers will also be rightly concerned with securing adequate recruitment and retention in the public service occupations.

Unfortunately, much of the policy debate is dominated by the unhelpful and ill-defined concept of the 'knowledge economy'. Work commissioned by SEEDA (Huggins, 2001 and 2003) defined it so narrowly as to include only a handful of hi-technology manufacturing and service activities, excluding vast swathes of economic activity, including business and financial services. This is a startling omission given that this is one of the obvious areas of comparative advantage of the UK economy and especially that of the Greater South East. Any set of international comparisons based on poor definitions will yield misleading results.[2]

The OECD uses a more inclusive definition of the knowledge economy, which includes hi-technology manufacturing and service activities, financial and business services, and health and education (OECD, 2003). These activities typically amount to around two-fifths of total employment in the advanced industrial economies. Other approaches use the proportion of graduates employed within sectors to define them as 'knowledge-intensive', though this leads to the obvious problem that, as the supply of graduates increases, more sectors will end up being defined as knowledge-intensive, even if their other characteristics have not changed.

The key question to ask is why would we want to define sectors that could be classified as knowledge-intensive anyway? Presumably it is so we can target them for some

---

2   On this definition neither a think tank nor an accountancy firm would be regarded as being part of the knowledge economy.

kind of special attention from public policy, in which case it sounds like the 21st Century equivalent of an industrial policy based on 'picking winners', an approach that, by common agreement, had little success in the second half of the 20th Century, but which is still influential in the approach of many public agencies. If the 'knowledge economy' is to have any relevance to public policy, it will be by helping us to think further about what is going on in the labour market and what that might mean for policies in relation to employment, and education and training and how best to promote research and development. It should not be used to resurrect a sectoral approach to industrial policy, given spurious credibility by the use of 21st Century language.

Policy conclusions

We started this chapter with three key observations: first, the South East is one of the most prosperous regions within the UK and the EU; second, there are, however, serious disparities in prosperity within the region; third, there are also serious disparities in economic performance across the regions of the UK.

The Government has come to recognise that tackling economic inactivity and increasing employment rates is of key importance in narrowing regional disparities in the UK. It is also of key importance in narrowing disparities in prosperity within the South East. The key question for agencies and authorities within the South East is to understand what they might do to help address this agenda.

The economically inactive across the UK and in the South East are heterogeneous in nature. There are two overlapping groups which are of the greatest importance in terms of numbers: older members of the potential workforce and those inactive due to sickness and disability. Another important group are people with heavy caring responsibilities, including not only lone parents, who have been the focus of a lot of policy, but also carers of elderly and/or disabled relatives. Many of these carers will be looking for part-time and flexible employment opportunities that fit with their wider responsibilities. A relatively high proportion of those across these different groups may also be among the less-well qualified and those with poor basic skills.

The Government has launched a plethora of initiatives aimed at these groups, including the various 'new deals'. The range of services offered to these groups to help them back into work are the primary responsibility of Jobcentre Plus, which in many ways is likely to be the most important of the 'economic' agencies in the years ahead. Important initiatives going forward will be proposed reforms to the benefits system for those inactive due to sickness and disability, and the employment programmes that might build upon the current Pathways to Work pilots aimed at this group along with associated services, relating, for example, to rehabilitation.

However, the importance of the need to join up various supporting services from the point of view of the individual seeking to gain employment, raises the critical issue of how different agencies co-ordinate their work. This could be one of the key challenges facing local authorities, charged with enhancing the economic, social and environmental wellbeing of their populations. In developing their responsibilities for children's services, and for care services for adults and the elderly, local authorities could take the lead in bringing together other agencies like the Primary Care Trusts alongside Jobcentre Plus, the Learning and Skills Council and other stakeholders, to address some of the barriers which prevent people from securing sustained employment. As already emphasised, a key issue here is not only childcare services, but also care services for older relatives, structured so that people can work flexibly, and rehabilitation services. The boundaries between health and social care that have always thrown up difficult issues will pose further challenges in relation to support for people economically inactive due to sickness and disability.

The Local Strategic Partnerships, which local authorities often lead on, may find that inactivity and employment become a more useful way of focusing a key part of their agenda, rather than 'regeneration' per se. A good example of this is the Kent Partnership, formed in 2002. Kent's proposed Local Area Agreement, which will run from 2005-2008, includes a strategic partnership with the Department for Work and Pensions (DWP) at Ministerial/County Leader level, to go further than the current pilots designed to tackle employment problems (Kent, 2005).

Another policy area that would seem to require some joined-up working is transport. As will be discussed further in chapter 4, two important issues are first, identifying the transport infrastructure projects that could best contribute to boosting economic activity within a particular area and second, how public transport could be improved to help link areas where employment rates are low with areas where the labour market might be more buoyant. Both of these issues are relevant to the coastal areas within the South East where employment rates are lowest. Again, it is local authorities who are likely to take the lead on this with other relevant agencies.

The other obvious policy area that is thrown up is in relation to learning opportunities for disadvantaged adults. More than anywhere else this is where the plethora of agencies and initiatives is arguably most problematic. The key issue here is how far future funding will be routed directly through employers, how far through various 'planning' bodies including the Regional Skills Partnerships, and how far disadvantaged individuals will be allowed to choose learning opportunities for themselves – the option that would fit best with the general mantra in public service reform of allowing for more personal choice.

Clearly, policy-makers in the region will also want to play their part in the debate we need to have about adjusting our expectations of working life, in the context of increased longevity. For half the adult population the change in the state pension age will mean that, between 2010 and 2020, they will have to change their expectations of when they will be able to exit the workforce. As this should have a bigger effect on increasing the employment rate in the region than any other measure, authorities and agencies within the region need to be thinking now about how they will be supporting older adults, and especially women, to adjust to these changes.

One type of policy not suggested as a high priority would be the use of resources to support 'knowledge-intensive' sectors in the region's most prosperous areas, a strategy which anyway seems doomed to repeat past policy errors relating to sectoral-based industrial policy. Indeed, given the need for extra resources to support the employment agenda, the Government may well want agencies and authorities to think about how they allocate resources across different functions.

Tackling economic inactivity and improving employment would be of critical importance to the aim of reducing disparities in prosperity within the region, and this in turn would be the best means of maintaining the overall position of the region as one of the most successful regions within the UK and the EU. However, the region also has an interest in the less prosperous regions improving their employment rates and relative levels of output per head. As they have the most pressing problems to tackle in terms of economic inactivity, a focus on the employment agenda should help them to narrow the gap in prosperity with the better performing regions, including the South East. They simply have further to travel in boosting their employment rates. Their success would ease pressures on development and natural resources in the South East, by making other UK regions more attractive places to work and live.

The determination within government to address the employment issue and to address regional disparities in economic performance would be best served by reformulating the PSA target that relates to regional economic performance. A suggested alternative for the 2006 Spending Review would be:

> Over the long term reduce the persistent gap in output per head between the UK's regions by concentrating effort on increasing the growth rate in the lagging regions (with a particular focus on employment)

For the South East region this would mean voicing support for the efforts of the less prosperous regions, individually and collectively, to tackle their economic problems and particularly their relatively low employment rates. Within the South East, the priority would be to tackle those pockets of relatively low employment that exist within the region. A more equitable spread of economic activity across the UK and within the South East would be in everyone's interest.

Key findings

The South East's economic performance

- The South East is one of the UK's most prosperous regions and appears to be the only UK region with an above average trend growth rate.

- The economic performance of the South East compares well with what are generally regarded as the EU's most prosperous substantive regions, containing all the well known centres of commerce in Europe outside of London and Paris.

- There are, however, serious disparities in prosperity within the region, with certain groups (for example, people with disabilities) and certain areas (for example, Thanet) continuing to have relatively low levels of employment.

- There are also serious disparities in economic performance across the regions of the UK, which are not diminishing.

- The labour market in the South East is relatively tight but it is not overheating and there are still uncomfortable levels of labour market exclusion for some groups.

- Skill shortages and skills gaps do not seem to be a bigger problem in the South East than in other English regions and are not getting worse.

Economic policy in the South East

- No-one in the region appears to be arguing for an increased rate of growth in the South East, as would be required to meet the Government's current PSA target for narrowing regional disparities.

- The Government has an ambitious target for 80 per cent of adults aged 16-64 to be in work, compared with about 73 per cent currently in the UK and 77 per cent in the South East.

- If employment could be significantly raised within the region there would be less need for significantly higher levels of in-migration, with important consequences for the rate of growth of housing required within the region.

- There needs to be a balance between in-migration and mobilising the labour supply within the region to meet future labour demand.

- This will require a range of policy instruments to help older workers, the disabled and carers into employment, with better joining up of the relevant agencies and authorities within the region.

- One type of policy not suggested as a high priority would be the use of resources to support 'knowledge-intensive' sectors in the region's most prosperous areas, a strategy which anyway seems doomed to repeat past policy errors relating to sectoral-based industrial policy.

3: Meeting housing need in the South East

Introduction

Housing faces the same set of issues as any other area of public policy in terms of how to set priorities between competing objectives given constraints on resources. Since 1997, government policy has evolved around at least eight separate objectives, all with significant implications for resources: improving the standard of the existing housing stock; reducing homelessness; increasing the rate of build of social housing; more low-cost homeownership; addressing low housing demand in the 'North'; addressing housing shortages in the 'South'; reforming rents and housing benefit; and improving affordability.

Recent policy debate has focused around two particular issues: delivering a 'step change' in housing provision, mainly focused in the Greater South East, and broadening homeownership. Three documents are particularly relevant here. First, the Sustainable Communities Plan (ODPM, 2003) outlined plans to revive housing markets in some northern areas – through a combination of demolition and measures to increase these areas' attractiveness – and increase the supply of housing in key growth areas in southern England. Second, the Barker Review of Housing Supply (Barker, 2004) – jointly commissioned by HM Treasury and the ODPM – is a potentially ambitious agenda to drive down the trend rate of increase in real house prices, so as to improve the affordability of housing overall in the UK and regionally by significantly increasing output, especially of private housing. Third, the Five-Year Plan for housing (ODPM, 2005a) included various measures to extend homeownership among social and private renters as well as Key Workers, through the greater provision of low-cost homeownership schemes.

Alongside these debates another has occured over the public resources dedicated towards housing and associated areas such as transport. The Barker Review (2004), for example, did not report any detailed analysis in relation to the infrastructure costs associated with increased housebuilding. Meanwhile, the public debate on housing policy is stuck between a mixture of very big but essentially meaningless numbers like the £38 billion price tag attached to the Sustainable Communities Plan (ODPM, 2003) and the very small numbers attached to specific initiatives like the range of £3-20 million in public subsidy for the Homebuy scheme to help tenants buy part of their home (Gardiner, 2005).

What the UK needs is an open debate about whether, as a nation, we are prepared to devote the resources necessary to deliver these housing policy objectives and to meet other demands for improved infrastructure in areas such as transport. Figure 1 shows that housing saw a very sharp decline in public spending as a proportion of GDP from the early 1990s and through the first three/four years of the Labour Government (transport infrastructure issues are considered in chapter 4). Recent spending reviews should result in public spending on housing increasing as a proportion of GDP by the middle of the current decade back to the levels of the middle part of the last decade, but with spending still significantly lower than at the time of the 1992 election. Will it really be possible to deliver an ambitious housing policy agenda with public resources at two-thirds of the level of national income that were being devoted in the early 1990s?

Figure 1: Public spending on housing as a percentage of GDP, 1989-2008

Figure 1: Public spending on housing as a percentage of GDP, 1989-2008

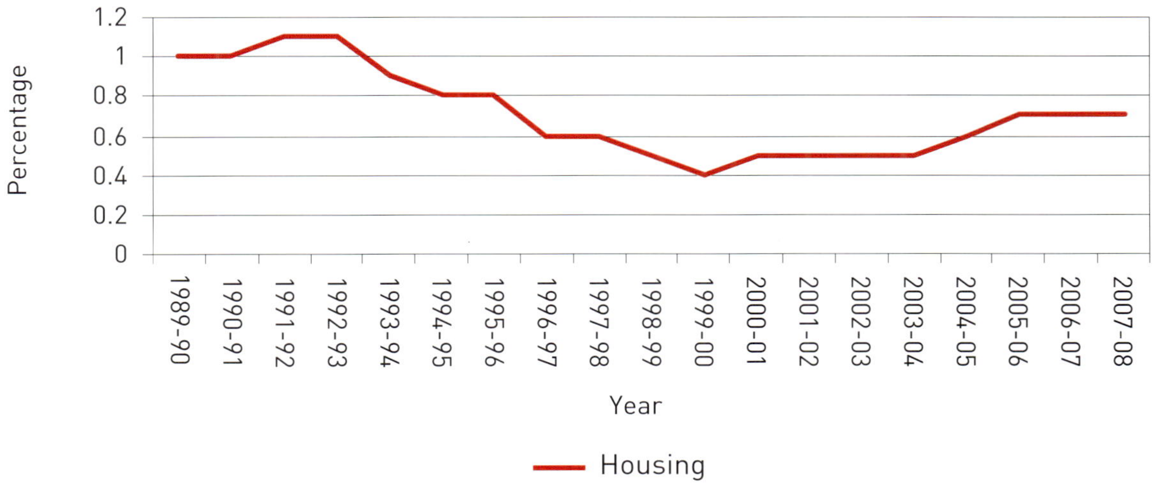

Source: Public Expenditure Statistical Analyses, HM Treasury, 2005

Drawing on work commissioned from Glen Bramley (2005) on demographic trends and affordability issues, this chapter will outline the demographic projections for the South East, identifying the South East's close inter-relationship with London as a key issue. The chapter will then move on to consider housing needs in the South East. Recent years have witnessed a significant increase in the number of households living in temporary accommodation. Additionally, the South East is England's second least affordable region for first time buyers. What is the most appropriate public policy response to these issues? This chapter will argue these needs should be met through an increased provision of affordable housing – both socially rented and low cost home-ownership schemes. The chapter will finally move on to argue that providing more affordable housing in the South East will require increased public spending, that new developments can be delivered sustainably but must adhere to the highest environmental standards, and will suggest governance reforms to encourage development in a more appropriate way.

Demographic trends and projections

England as a whole has been experiencing fairly strong population growth in recent years, with most growth concentrated in southern regions. Figure 2 shows that between 1991 and 2003 all English regions, with the exception of the North East and North West, experienced population growth. Figure 2 also provides population projections up to 2028, with all regions, except again the North East, expected to grow between 2003 and 2028. Between 1991 and 2003, the South East was second to London in absolute population growth. Between 2003 and 2028, however, the South East is projected to be the fastest growing region in England. Overall, the southern regions incorporating the South East as well as London, the South West, the East and the East Midlands, are projected to receive the bulk of English population growth between 2003 and 2028 (82.4 per cent).

Demographic projections are very sensitive to the assumptions used. These current sub-national population projections are based on recent trends in migration, and births and deaths related to regional age structures. The measurement of international migration is particularly problematic, due to sample sizes, the reliability of data and the contingent nature of international migration and asylum flows. All projections should, therefore, be treated with caution as they are simply (albeit relatively sophisticated) extrapolations from recent trends.

Figure 2: Population by English region, 1991-2028

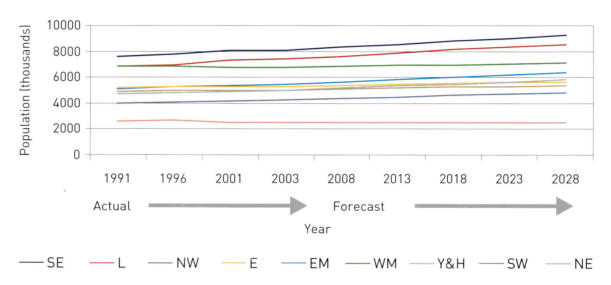

Source: Bramley, 2005 drawing on ONS data

The South East has been a consistent high growth region in terms of household numbers. It has gained more than a million extra households, an increase of nearly a half (46 per cent), since 1971. Projecting future household numbers is a difficult exercise, not least because of data limitations, but also because household growth is contingent upon a number of variables.

Again highlighting problems with housing data, recent revisions to the level of household formation have revised *downwards* the expected new household formation in the South East. Over the 20 year period from 2001-21, the projected increase in households in the South East has dropped modestly from 712,000 to 677,000. London's projected household increase has been revised significantly upwards. The number of households in London is expected to increase by 927,000 between 2001-21. The demographic inter-relationship between London and the South East will be returned to below.

Table 1 shows annual household growth for the decade 2001-2011. Both the previous (1999) and interim revised (2004) figures are presented. Table 1 also presents the actual past level of household formation in each English region for 1991-2003. There are three points of particular interest here. First, the South East is projected to grow by 32,400 households a year between 2001 and 2011. Second, that despite the downward revision, household growth in the South East between 2001 and 2011 is still expected to be higher than during the period from 1991 to 2003. Third, the effect of the upward revision in London is again obvious, with annual household growth projected to be 48,300 between 2001 and 2011, up from previous projections of 20,700.

Again highlighting the limitations of housing data, the Greater London Authority (GLA) and ONS have different projections for London's future household growth. The GLA have argued that ONS' figure of 48,300 is too high because it is not compatible with the number of households recorded in London in the 2001 Census. The GLA estimate that the figure of 34,000 – as presented in the London Plan (GLA, 2004) – is more appropriate. Some, for example Bramley (2005), have argued that the GLA's figure should be treated sceptically.

Table 1: Projected annual household growth 2001-2011, compared with actual past growth

Region	Previous (1999)	Interim (2004)	Actual Past (1991-2003)
North East	6,200	3,100	4,768
Yorks & Humber	17,500	13,100	9,126
North West	17,500	15,900	13,056
East Midlands	16,900	16,100	16,812
West Midlands	14,100	14,700	13,623
South West	21,900	22,200	20,810
East	23,500	23,300	22,144
South East	38,700	32,400	27,286
London	20,700	48,300	17,957
England	176,900	188,900	145,582

Source: Bramley, 2005 drawing on DETR, 1999; ODPM, 2004a; and HSSA returns to local authorities

Scratching beneath these aggregate figures, the drivers of population change and household formation are very important to any debates around housing numbers. There are two ways in which a given area's population can change: either natural change (births minus deaths) or net migration. Figure 3 presents the balance of these different drivers of population change for selected English regions or groups of regions. In 2003-04 the biggest driver of population growth for the South East (and the East) was positive net migration. Natural change contributed around 14,000 of the South East's population increase, with the remaining two-thirds (28,000) due to migration.

London stands out for having natural change that is strongly positive and net migration that is negative. This does not conform with the stereotype of London as the dominant city sucking in migrants from home and abroad, although it does experience large gross inflows. In common with many other cities, London is losing more population through out-migration than it is gaining through in-migration. In particular, it is losing older adults and families. This is significant because London has a close relationship with the South East. The South East (and to a lesser extent the East of England and other parts of the southern regions) is the region to which migrants leaving London are most likely to go. According to ONS figures, in 2002-03 the South East received 36.5 per cent of all out-migration from London. The amount of migration in and out of London to surrounding regions suggests it has a significant effect on the

Figure 3: Components of population change by region and group of region, 2003-4

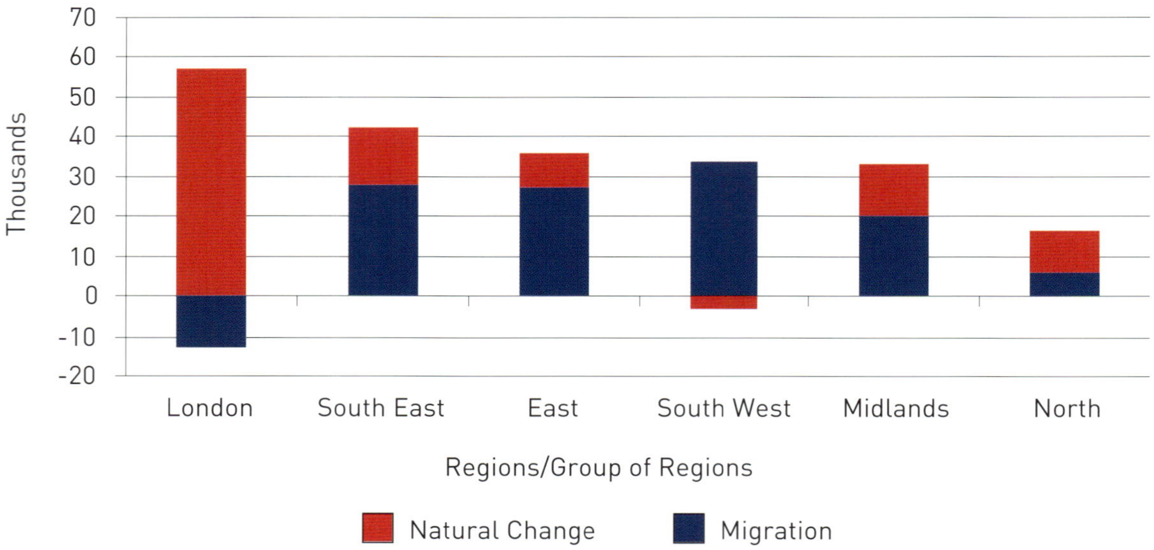

Source: Bramley, 2005 drawing on ONS data

whole interregional migration and housing system. As Figure 4 highlights, this is especially so for the South East. Other than a slight net balance with the East, London is the only region that is a net contributor of population to the South East. In 2002-03 nearly 100,000 people moved from London into the South East, producing a net migration flow of 46,500. The other surprising finding from these data is that in 2002-03 the South East was a net loser of population through internal migration to all other regions (except the East and London, as mentioned above).

Figure 4: Internal migration flows into and out of the South East by origin/destination, 2002-03

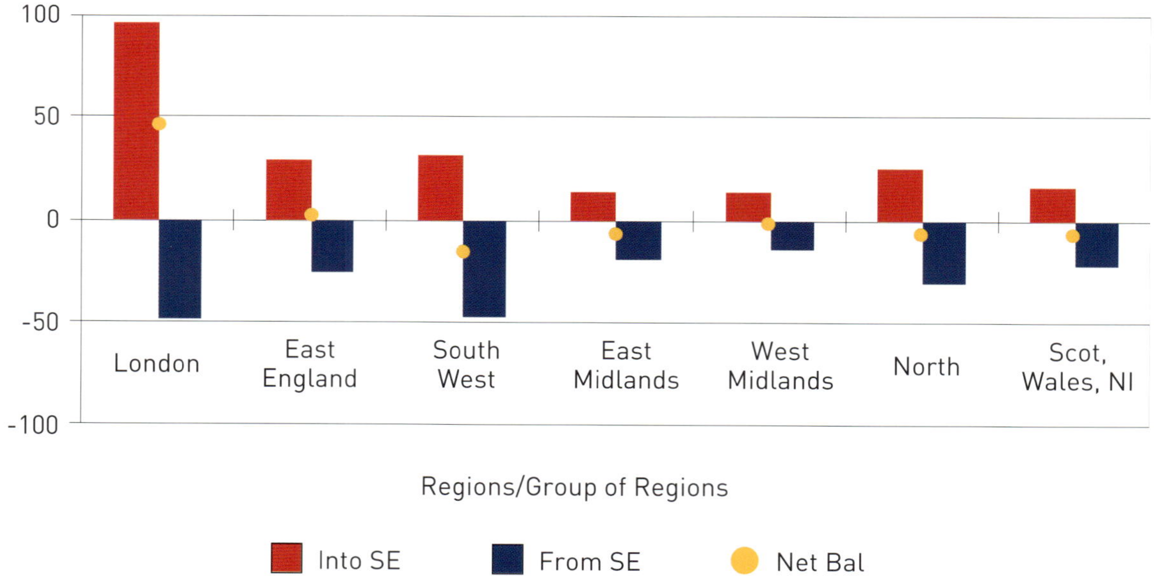

Source: Bramley, 2005 drawing on ONS data

As well as internal migration, it is also important to consider the role of international migration in recent and projected population change. International migration has become much more important in the last decade in driving UK population and household growth. Gross international in-migration doubled in the decade to 2002, to over half a million. While out-migration increased as well, the net balance has shifted from an approximate balance in the early 1990s to a net annual gain of 150-170,000 in the most recent two years for which we have figures (2001 and 2002). In the four years to 2002, international migration contributed approximately 80 per cent of the UK's annual population increase.

London is the dominant destination for international migrants – 70 per cent of net inflow – and this has clearly contributed to London's increasingly buoyant population numbers. The share of the South East is more modest, averaging 11 per cent of net inflows, although this is still of some significance for the region. Perhaps more important is the indirect effect via London, as international migration adds to the pressure in the capital which then is reflected subsequently in an out-migration cascade effect.

ONS data suggests that migration – especially from London and international migration flows – accounts for two-thirds of the South East's population change, and natural change one-third. The *South East Plan: Consultation Draft* presents a different balance for household growth based on modelling produced by Anglia Polytechnic University. The *South East Plan: Consultation Draft* is working on the assumption that household growth over the plan period will be driven by 'one-third […] net in-migration into the region [and] the remainder from internally generated needs' (SEERA, 2005). It is difficult to wholly reconcile these two different results. However, two factors suggest they are not incompatible. First, in-migrants to the South East tend to be young families, and therefore whilst they would register as two or more individuals in population change terms, they would only represent one household. Second, trends in household composition, particularly the growth in single person households (especially between the ages of 45 and 64), suggests that existing residents may have a larger impact than in-migrants.

The link between London and the South East does, however, present a difficult political issue. The inter-relationship between both regions is important to their mutual prosperity. But if London is unable to meet its own housebuilding needs, should the South East necessarily be expected to fill the gap through increased housebuilding?

Housing priorities

Housing need

Holmans et al. (2004) identify housing need as a normative concept derived from housing policy aims, such as 'a decent home for everyone'. The Government has, for example, committed to ensuring that, by 2010, all social housing meets the Decent Homes Standard. There is also an aim to increase the proportion of private housing occupied by vulnerable groups in decent condition (ODPM, 2005a). Beyond the quality of the housing stock there are two issues that could be identified as representing particular housing needs. First, those unintentionally homeless and in temporary accommodation. Second, the backlog of housing need.

The 'unintentionally homeless'

The 'flow' of those accepted as unintentionally homeless by local authorities has increased in recent years at the national level.[3] Between 1991 and 1997, the national figure dropped quite substantially. Since 1997, however, there has been a steady rise, with a particularly steep rise in 2002-2003, due in part to a legislative change that increased the number of unintentionally homeless categories. By 2003, the national figure had returned to the 1991 level (137,250 and 137,220, respectively). The South East, by contrast, has shown a steady increase, with the 2003 figure ten per cent higher than that for 1991.

Significantly, at both the regional (South East) and national level, this flow of unintentially homeless has recently translated into an increase in the *stock* of households in temporary accommodation. Figure 5 presents the number of households in temporary accommodation – specifically those accepted by local authorities as being homeless and who cannot be immediately placed in social, or other appropriate, housing. As Figure 5 shows, again after an initial drop in the early 1990s, the national figure has grown significantly between 1996 and 2003, with London the dominant driver. The South East and other 'high demand' regions (the East, the South West and the East Midlands) also account for a significant proportion. In 2003, the South East had 13,300 households in temporary accommodation. The increased flow and stock of homeless households can arguably be attributed to a combination of two factors. First, the increase in the flow of homeless acceptances. Second, a slowing in the level of overall housebuilding, particularly social housing (this is discussed further below; see also Figure 6).

Figure 5: Households in temporary accommodation by selected English region, 1991-2003

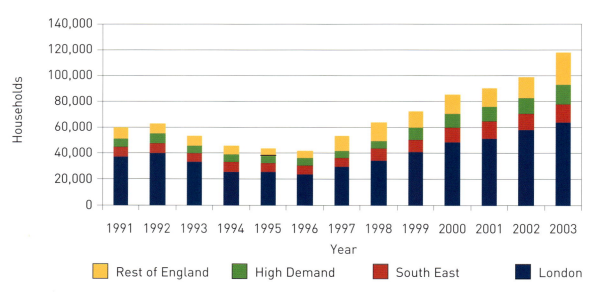

Source: Wilcox, 2004 and other data direct from ODPM (via email)

Notes: From 1997 the data contains 'homeless at home' (households accepted as homeless but who remain in their existing accommodation pending rehousing). The homeless at home data is unavailable at a regional level before this. The homeless at home figure for the final quarter of each year has been used and the 2003 figure is provisional.

3 Households are considered homeless if they: have no home in the UK or anywhere else in the world; have no home where they can live together with their immediate family; can only stay where they are on a very temporary basis; don't have permission to live where they are; have been locked out of home and aren't allowed back; can't live at home because of violence or threats of violence which are likely to be carried out against them or someone in their household; can't afford to stay where they are; live in a vehicle or boat and have nowhere to put it; or, it isn't reasonable for them to stay in their home for any reason (for example, if their home is in very poor condition).

The backlog of housing need

There are a number of different sources on the backlog of housing need. It is a contested area, with different calculations including (or excluding) different groups as representing a backlog of housing need. The point of highlighting these figures is to show that housing need does exist beyond households in temporary accommodation. It is of course a value judgement as to which groups represent housing need.

Bramley (2005), for example, calculates the backlog of housing need through an analysis of local authority waiting list data for social housing. Between 2000 and 2003 this data reveals a universal increase in waiting lists in all English regions. Within the South East specifically, Bramley estimates a backlog of the order of 72-97,000 individuals with housing needs.

In work commissioned by SEERA, Holmans (2004) suggests the backlog of housing need in the South East in 2001 was 28,500 households (in contrast to Bramley's (2005) calculation of individuals in need). The calculations are presented in Table 2. It is important to note that SEERA's figure is a conservative one. It excludes homeless households in private rented accommodation and 'other accommodation' as not being important to the backlog because it does not necessarily require new dwellings to meet the need. Holmans (2004) calculates this figure to be 99,000 households. This higher figure is more in line with Holmans et al.'s (2004) work for Shelter, which calculated the backlog of unmet need in England to be 950,000 households, 650,000 of which would have to be met through additions to the current housing stock. Unfortunately, this report did not provide regional breakdowns of this aggregate figure.

Table 2: The backlog of unmet housing need in the South East, 2001

Category of 'backlog'	Number
(1) Bed and breakfast, hostels and refuges	2,800
(2) Other accomm. arranged by local authorities under homelessness legislation	8,800
(3) Concealed families preferring separate accomm.	9,000
(4) Sharing households in the private rented sector preferring separate accomm.	16,700
Total	37,300
Total excluding category 2	28,500

Source: Holmans, 2004

Housing demand

Holmans et al. (2004) define housing demand as 'effective demand in the market for housing of adequate standard to buy or to rent'.

The South East is generally the second least affordable region within England

A significant proportion of the South East's population face housing affordability problems. Table 3 presents figures for the English regions in 2002. Measures of affordability vary according to which methodology is used, so this is a particularly useful table as it compares different models, revealing broadly similar results. The first data column shows the average percentage of under-35 year old households able to buy at threshold entry prices (lower quartile price), as population-weighted regional averages of local authority level estimates generated by the Bramley (2005) model. The second column shows the Bramley model results for working under-35 households only. The third column presents a different model, which is used in the Joseph Rowntree Foundation's 'Can Work, Can't Buy' reports (Wilcox, 2003). The next two columns compare Bramley's model with direct estimates made within the Family Resources Survey micro-dataset, using the same local house prices but estimating affordability at a sub-regional level (fourth column) and district level (fifth column) using actual reported incomes and household composition for sample households. The near-universal conclusion from these models is that the South East is England's second least affordable region.

Table 3: Affordability rates by region, comparing Bramley model with Wilcox, FRS and IMD index 2002 to show percent of target households able to buy

Region	Model All <35	Model Working <35	Wilcox Working	FRS based	IMD Index
North	52.7	66.5	76.9	54.8	54.8
Yorks & Humber	53.1	65.1	75.9	52.8	52.7
North West	53.1	66.4	75.1	54.1	54.0
East Midlands	50.2	60.7	57.9	50.4	50.5
West Midlands	45.6	56.6	64.0	51.0	51.5
South West	35.4	43.0	31.5	37.1	37.3
East	39.1	47.7	41.3	41.1	42.1
South East	34.1	42.1	35.8	35.0	35.3
London	21.7	29.0	24.5	24.4	24.7
England	41.1	50.9	50.8	42.8	43.0

Sources: Bramley & Karley, forthcoming; Wilcox, 2003; IMD, 2004

The levels of affordability must, however, be put in the context of the market cycle. Table 4 presents the changes in affordability through time based on Bramley's (2005) model. The general picture emerging is that affordability improved from the late 1980s (previous boom) into the early and middle 1990s, but then deteriorated in the later 1990s and early 2000s, to a level worse than in the previous boom. While the broad ranking of regions has remained similar, affordability deteriorated markedly more in the South East and in the South West (see also Wilcox, 2003), while in London conditions at the end of the period were similar to those in the late 1980s. Importantly, however, the future affordability projections suggest the situation in England as a whole, and in the South East, will improve, with measures of affordability returning very closely to the levels of the period 1986-91. In other words, the housing market will adjust, with a period of falling or stagnant house prices making houses more affordable again. However, the South East will remain the second least affordable region after London, but with the South West and the East experiencing similar problems of affordability. So, although the problem of affordability will *not* have generally got worse across the cycle, England as a whole and the South East as a region will still face problems in meeting housing needs and demands.

Table 4: Proportion of under-35 households able to buy by English region, 1986-2009

Region	1986-91[1]	1991[2]	1997[3]	2001[4]	2002[5]	2004[6]	2006[6]	2009[6]
North	56.3	53.4	54.1	50.6	49.6	50.2	54.3	57.7
Yorks & Humber	53.8	55.5	56.1	50.4	44.0	50.5	55.0	58.6
North West	58.4	53.1	54.2	50.3	47.6	50.4	54.8	58.3
East Midlands	64.6	62.9	63.6	48.1	40.2	46.7	52.2	56.1
West Midlands	47.0	55.6	54.0	42.3	35.3	43.8	49.2	53.0
South West	41.5	57.1	52.5	33.2	24.2	34.6	40.8	45.0
East	53.2	59.7	55.9	38.6	30.8	35.3	41.7	46.0
South East	**42.9**	59.9	48.3	31.6	26.8	31.8	38.2	**42.7**
London	17.6	38.1	22.5	22.4	20.2	20.4	25.2	28.8
England	45.8	55.0	49.6	38.8	33.6	38.7	44.1	48.0

Sources: [1] Bramley, 1996; [2] Bramley and Smart, 1995; [3] Bramley, 1998; [4] & [5] Housing Corporation, 2003; [6] Bramley, 2005

Note: 1986-2002 results are from different studies using different assumptions but similar methodologies; 2004-2009 includes a 'wealth adjustment'

How to address these affordability problems is currently one of the most contentious debates within housing policy. The Barker Review (2004) argues that supply must better respond to affordability needs, with a significant increase in the output of new housing required. Barker argues that an additional 141,000 dwellings a year over current targets would reduce real house price growth to 1.1 per cent per annum (against an average of 2.4-2.7 per cent since 1970). It also argues that regional affordability indicators should be established, so that housing supply can more adequately respond in each region, to maintain this lower level of house price inflation.

However, there are a number of reasons why the Barker Review's methodology does not seem an appropriate way of approaching housing affordability issues. Firstly, with trend real incomes also growing at around 2.5 per cent per annum, it is unclear why the 2.4-2.7 per cent rate of real house price inflation would create an overall problem of affordability for the UK, even if affordability is a problem for some households. Secondly, as well as showing that affordability will not worsen across the market cycle, Bramley (2005) argues that the Barker figure of an extra 141,000 dwellings a year, to reduce real price growth to 1.1 per cent per annum, is too high. Instead, reporting the results of modelling undertaken with Chris Leishman, Bramley (2005) argues that an extra 59,000 houses could have the same effect. The significant disparity between these two figures would seem to call into question whether it really is possible for policymakers to set targets for output in the housing market to achieve a particular path for house price inflation, in order to meet targets for affordability at the national or regional level. Such an approach seems a blunt and probably ineffective tool in a complex market and one, moreover, subject to speculative pressures.

This said, building on the evidence of the increase in the stock of homeless households in temporary accommodation presented in Figure 5, it is clear that there is a need for increased affordable housing in the South East and a demand for increased intermediate provision.

The need for affordable housing

Table 5 shows the results of the Bramley (2005) model annual needs calculation by region over the projection period. The results presented are both historical and a future projection. This assessment includes an allowance for reducing the backlog (based on discounted waiting lists) by ten per cent per year, an allowance for net migration and for older owner-occupiers needing to move into social renting. For the South East, the numbers rise from 38,218 in 2002 to 43,526 in 2004, then fall back to 33,536 by 2009.

Table 5: Net positive new need for affordable housing 2002-09, units per annum

Region	2002	2004	2006	2009	Average
North East	434	848	703	625	653
Yorks & Humber	2,722	5,270	4,387	3,594	3,993
North West	3,975	6,996	5,701	4,689	5,340
East Midlands	5,541	9,290	7,777	6,795	7,351
West Midlands	5,493	8,759	7,186	5,949	6,847
South West	21,789	26,056	23,336	21,241	23,106
East	17,097	22,369	19,494	17,459	19,105
South East	38,218	43,526	38,241	33,536	38,380
London	49,047	53,758	48,596	40,932	48,083
England	144,315	176,873	155,422	134,821	152,858

Source: Bramley, 2005

There is also a clear demand for an increase in the provision of intermediate housing.[4] Table 6 shows the results of this assessment of the potential need/demand for Low Cost Home Ownership (LCHO) by region for 2002, drawn from Bramley's modelling for the Home Ownership Task Force. It models the two main schemes: shared ownership (SO) of a new unit, assuming a 40 per cent tranche purchased (the average in practice); and 75 per cent Homebuy of a second-hand unit at threshold entry price level. The first two columns show the percentage of new (under-35) households able to afford these two options, but not outright purchase. Overall, 11.5 per cent extra households could afford shared ownership, and 12.2 per cent could afford Homebuy. It should be noted that these are cumulative figures and households may be counted under both schemes. Whichever is the higher figure reveals the overall potential for affordable provision per region. There is a marked regional variation, particularly for shared ownership. The headline for the South East here, is that it is the region with the highest potential for LCHO schemes in 2002.

The third and fourth columns translate these figures into net need numbers, allowing for the net need position in each authority. This analysis shows that need is overwhelmingly concentrated in the southern regions, again particularly in London and the South East. The final two columns in Table 6 provide rough estimates of the additional potential annual demand that may exist among the stock of existing social and private renters,[5] with southern regions – and London and the South East especially – again demonstrating the highest figures.

---

4   Intermediate housing encompasses a range of housing provision, both rental and ownership. Two Low Cost Home Ownership (LCHO) schemes are used here. Shared Ownership – the buyer acquires a stake of between 25 per cent and 75 per cent of the market value and rents the remainder of the dwelling from a Registered Social Landlord (RSL) at a subsidised rate). And, Homebuy – the buyer acquires a 75 per cent stake and the balance of 25 per cent is funded initially by grant which takes the form of an 'equity loan' from an RSL, interest-free but repayable on subsequent sale at prevailing market values.

5   This is based on an analysis of the Survey of English Housing, taking percentages in the relevant affordability bands for each of seven broad types of local authority (distinguishing broad regions), and then applying these rates to the numbers of social and private tenants in each local authority. These are converted to annual flows by taking the rates of mobility out of these tenures into owner occupation, divided by the number of such tenant households who could afford to buy in the open market (again using the SEH).

Table 6: Potential additional Low Cost Home Ownership, by region, 2002

Region	SO % extra	Homebuy % extra	SO Need	Homebuy Need	Social Renters	Private Renters
North	3.7	6.5	46	96	1,079	1,204
Yorks & Humber	4.9	7.9	540	664	2,060	4,453
North West	4.9	7.6	823	961	3,243	5,788
East Midlands	8.9	10.8	1,455	1,612	2,027	4,167
West Midlands	9.5	11.2	1,257	1,453	2,690	4,435
South West	14.5	15.6	5,056	5,407	3,716	13,963
East	16.3	15.7	4,672	4,530	4,805	11,682
South East	17.3	16.5	9,806	9,299	6,260	20,660
London	15.7	13.5	9,492	8,248	6,655	24,906
England	11.5	12.2	33,148	32,271	32,536	91,258

Source: Bramley and Karley, forthcoming, based on work undertaken for the Home Ownership Task Force, Housing Corporation, 2003

This clear ongoing need for more affordable housing – both socially rented and inter-mediate – must also be viewed within the context of a significant decline in the provision of affordable housing. As Figure 6 identifies there has been a downward trend in housing completions in the UK since the mid-1960s. Recently, there is a drop in output identifiable after 1988-89 with the ending of the 'Lawson boom', with no strong trend since the early 1990s. The level of private housebuilding has remained relatively

Figure 6: Housing completions by tenure type, UK, 1949-2003

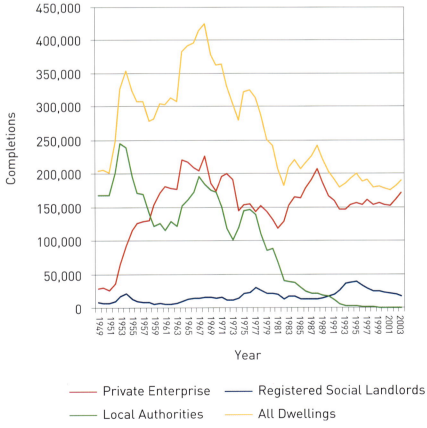

Source: ODPM, 2005b

stable since the late 1950s. The significant drop in total output can be most clearly attributed to the severe reduction in the number of social houses built, especially as local authority programmes ground to a halt, with the growth in the Registered Social Landlords (RSLs) sector only partly compensating.

Given the demonstrable need for affordable housing, the projected improvement in affordability for first time buyers through the decade, and the reservations over the Barker approach to improving affordability, an increase in the provision of affordable housing would be a more appropriate response to the South East's housing needs.

In the *South East Plan: Consultation Draft* three different targets for the annual output of new housing are presented: 25,500, 28,000 and 32,000 (these figures are explained in more detail in the appendix). Additionally, it is proposed that, of all new housebuilding during the plan period 2006-26, 25 per cent should be socially rented housing and ten-15 per cent should be intermediate housing. These figures reflect government recommendations. If the figure of 32,000 new dwellings a year – the highest figure used in SEERA's *South East Plan: Consultation Draft* – is used, then what increases in output are required to achieve these proportions of affordable housing?

Answering this question, however, highlights once again the problems with all housing data presented in this paper. ODPM and SEERA present different figures for both the overall dwellings completed in the South East and the proportion which has been provided by public subsidy. As presented in Table 7, the ODPM's figures on dwellings completed in the South East over the period from 1992-93 to 2004-05, suggests that an average of about 24,400 dwellings of all types were completed in the region each year, of which on average 3,800 were provided with public subsidy (and therefore 20,600 without subsidy). The data on the split between social and intermediate housing is not available.

Table 7: Permanent dwellings completed by tenure for the South East, 1992-93 to 2004-05

| | ODPM | | SEERA | |
	All Dwellings	Housing provided by public subsidy	All Dwellings	Housing provided by public subsidy (social rental/ shared ownership)
1990/91	29,867	5,482	No data	
1991/92	27,373	4,183	29,093	
1992/93	24,040	4,579	25,508	
1993/94	25,797	5,276	26,452	
1994/95	26,955	4,931	28,146	
1995/96	26,992	5,272	29,084	
1996/97	25,048	3,656	27,489	
1997/98	25,441	4,099	28,747	
1998/99	23,346	3,672	26,536	
1999/00	23,077	2,889	25,502	
2000/01	21,839	2,818	23,177	
2001/02	21,813	2,900	25,417	4,602 (3,737/865)
2002/03	22,726	2,781	24,674	4,148 (3,520/628)
2003/04	24,263	3,245	28,212	4,592 (3,842/750)
2004/05	25,829	3,512	No data	No data

Sources: SEERA, 2004 drawing on P2m returns from local authorities; returns from National Housebuilding Council (NHBC), ODPM, 2004b and ODPM 2005c; LA returns for total completions. Also Housing Corporation outturn statements 2002, 2003, 2004 for social unit completions

SEERA's figures on the other hand suggest that overall housing completions and the number of dwellings provided by public subsidy are higher than ODPM reports. As Table 7 indicates, SEERA's figures suggest the South East has been building more dwellings overall from the early 1990s, and more social housing from 2000 (the start of available data) than the figures from ODPM. On average, 26,600 dwellings have been completed each year since 1992-93, with an average of 4,400 of these dwellings built with public subsidy over the period from 2001-02 to 2003-04.

Taking the 32,000 figure in the *South East Plan: Consultation Draft* as an example, 25 per cent of the total would equate to 8,000 units of social housing. A further ten-15 per cent intermediate housing would amount to 3,200-4,800 dwellings. So out of the overall figure of 32,000, between 11,200 and 12,800 would need to be provided with some form of public subsidy, leaving between 19,200 and 20,800 to be built without subsidy. Over the last decade, the private sector has already delivered an average of 20,600 dwellings annually without subsidy (see Table 8). So, put together ODPM's actual housebuilding numbers with SEERA's assumptions about the proportion in the future requiring public subsidy (and use the target of 32,000 dwellings a year) and the striking conclusion is that *all* the extra dwellings in the South East would need to be social or intermediate forms of housing. About 7,600 extra dwellings provided with public subsidy annually would be consistent with the averages for private housebuilding achieved in the period up to 2004-05.

Table 8 also repeats these calculations for other recommended annual housebuilding rates in the South East. The third column presents the implications for affordable and private housing output, if SEERA's social and intermediate housing targets are applied to the SEERA officials' highest level of housebuilding recommended to the regional assembly. The fourth column does the same for Glen Bramley's (2005) recommendation of 41,000 new dwellings a year. The appendix also provides more detail on both of these housebuilding figure recommendations. Table 8 shows that, even with annual housebuilding outputs that represent significant increases over current levels, the amount of extra private housebuilding required would vary from ten to 25 per cent over current levels. This is significantly below Barker's recommendation of an approximate doubling of private housing output.

Table 8: Calculations of required housing outputs using SEERA's affordable housing targets and different overall annual output figures

	SE Plan highest figure	SEERA officials' highest recommendation	Bramley recommendation
Annual housebuilding output, all dwellings	32,000	36,000	41,000
Of which: 25% social housing	8,000	9,000	10,250
And: 10-15% intermediate housing	4,000	4,500	5,125
Therefore: private housebuilding	20,000	22,500	25,625
Average private housebuilding rate (last decade)	20,600	20,600	20,600
Average affordable housebuilding rate (last decade)	3,800	3,800	3,800
Additional affordable housing required	7,600	9,700	11,575
Additional private housebuilding required	N/A	1,900	5,025

Inevitably within public policy discussion, the cost implications of this increase in (affordable) housing provided through public subsidy must be considered. The 2004 Spending Review committed the Government to delivering 10,000 extra units of social housing a year by 2008. Despite the publication of the regional housing spending figures by the ODPM (2005d) at the end of March 2005, it is still not clear what proportion of these extra units will be built in the South East region. However, we can be fairly clear that most of these extra units will be in the Greater South East. If the South East's share is one-quarter of the total, that is about 2,500. Using the ODPM's figures, about one-third of the extra dwellings that need to be provided with public subsidy in the region (at an overall building rate of 32,000) might be funded from the commitments made in the 2004 Spending Review.

Above these resources already committed, how much would the additional dwellings built with public subsidy cost? Figures provided by Holmans et al. (2004) for Shelter suggest an average unit cost of about £65,000 in 2003-04 prices for a unit of social housing built in the South East. If the ODPM figures on housebuilding are more reliable, the extra 5,000 or so units required might cost up to £325 million. These figures are likely to be an overestimate as the costs of intermediate housing are likely to be lower, but we do not know the unit costs and/or what proportion of the extra dwellings would need to be intermediate (because we do not know the current split between social and intermediate housing).

It is important to emphasise that more affordable housing in the South East could be delivered by a range of providers. Private developers and housebuilders as well as local authorities and arms length management organisations are now able to bid for Housing Corporation grants under the New Partnerships in Affordable Housing pilot scheme, alongside the traditional RSLs (Housing Corporation, 2004). The whole affordable housing programme for 2006-08 is likely to be opened up for competition between providers.

It is also interesting to note the implications for affordable and private housebuilding rates of the *South East Plan: Consultation Draft*'s middle annual housebuilding figure – 28,000. As Scenario A in Table 9 demonstrates, if 28,000 new dwellings a year were built, to meet the targets for social and intermediate housing provision would mean a decrease in the private housebuilding rate to 17,500. Such a drop in the private housebuilding rate seems unlikely. Scenario B in Table 9 therefore identifies the implications for the output of social and intermediate housing if the private housebuilding rate at 20,600 is maintained. Under this scenario, the affordable housing targets of the *South East Plan: Consultation Draft* would not be met.

Table 9: The implications of a 28,000 annual housing growth rate for private and affordable housing outputs

Scenario A	Scenario B
To meet the proposed affordable housing targets.	To maintain the existing private housebuilding rate.
Proportion of private housingbuilding falls: 17,500	Rate of private housebuilding is maintained: 20,600
Proportion of affordable housing: 10,500 - 25% of output is social housing: 7,000 - 10-15% of output is intermediate housing: 3,500	Remaining housing: 7,400 - Two thirds of this figure is socially rented housing: around 4,900 - One third of this figure is intermediate housing: around 2,500

Note: The two-thirds and one-third proportions referred to under Scenario B reflect the split between the 25 per cent social housing and ten-15 per cent (calculated at 12.5 per cent) intermediate housing targets identified in the 'South East Plan: Consultation Draft'. Specifically, after the current private housebuilding figure is deducted from 28,000, the remaining figure is divided by three, with two-thirds of that figure going to social housing as it is twice the intermediate housing target (25 per cent compared to 12.5 per cent respectively).

Infrastructure costs and public spending

Increasing the provision of affordable housing in the South East will require more public resources. In overall aggregate terms, the Government seems to have dedicated significant public resources to delivering the Sustainable Communities agenda. Press releases after the 2004 Spending Review championed the ODPM's '£38 billion' budget, providing extra public spending on housing, including an extra 10,000 social homes a year by 2008 (a 50 per cent increase in provision) and a £200 million Community Infrastructure Fund (CIF) for transport investment.

However, as highlighted in Figure 1, public spending on housing and transport as a proportion of GDP is only returning to early- to mid-1990s levels because public capital programmes were cut back significantly through most of the 1990s. It has been very difficult to obtain detailed information from government over the expected costs associated with providing the necessary infrastructure for future housing growth. The ODPM has commissioned work to assess the local costs of delivering increased house-building, but this has not yet reported. There is also some scepticism over how extensive the work will be, even from within government.

This brings us back again to the central question of whether, as a nation, we are prepared to devote the resources that seem necessary to deliver a 'step change' in housing supply and associated infrastructure, and to meet the other objectives for housing policy. Compared to most other industrialised nations, the UK invests a small proportion of its GDP in residential buildings (see Figure 7).

Figure 7: International comparison of gross fixed investment in residential buildings as a percentage of GDP, 1985-2001

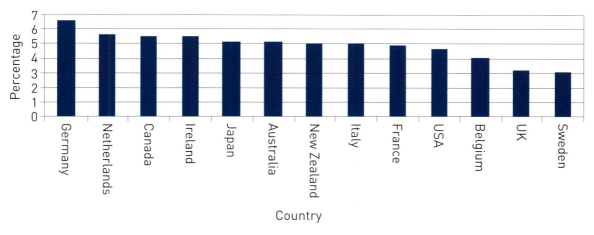

Source: Wilcox, 2004

Notes: 1) Gross fixed investment in dwellings and GDP are at market prices
2) Germany's figures refer to the Federal Republic before reunification for the years until 1990

Planning system contributions

The planning system itself is often seen as an opportunity to provide a significant number of affordable houses without public cost. Section 106 (of the Town and Country Planning Act 1990) agreements are seen as the key mechanism. As part of the granting of planning permission, and agreed in negotiation between the developer and local authority, developers are asked to contribute towards the broader costs of development, not simply affordable housing (for example, the provision of infrastructure).

Evidence provided in the two most comprehensive reviews of Section 106 argued that, while it is an increasingly important mechanism for delivering affordable housing, very little affordable housing is delivered without any public subsidy (Crook et al., 2002; Monk et al., 2005). In fact Monk et al. (2005) argue that the public cost per dwelling is similar whether Section 106 or Social Housing Grant (the public subsidy) is used. Additionally, and echoing Crook et al.'s (2002) earlier findings, Monk et al. (2005) suggest that of all the affordable homes provided through Section 106 nationally, only nine per cent – or 2,260 dwellings – did not receive some form of public grant.

Current planning system contributions are unlikely to meet the need for increased provision of affordable housing. It is unsurprising, therefore, that other mechanisms are being proposed. The Barker Review, for example, proposed that the Government should tax some of the windfall gains that landowners receive once their land is sold for residential development. Planning permission would be contingent on the payment of a 'Planning-gain Supplement' (PGS) that would provide 'additional resources to boost housing supply' (Barker, 2004). Government is currently investigating its desirability and practicability.

Additionally, there are other examples of emerging ideas to help fund new development. The South West of England Regional Development Agency have, for example, proposed the establishment of a revolving 'Regional Infrastructure Fund' (RIF) that 'would pay for infrastructure up-front and collect developer contributions through legal agreements when the profits begin to flow' (SWERDA, 2005). Recent press reports have also suggested that a special development tariff of up to £20,000 per new dwellings to be paid by developers to contribute towards local infrastructure needs, is planned for the Milton Keynes-South Midlands growth area (Planning Resource, 2005).

The Government is also consulting on other financing changes to enable both regional and local authorities more flexibility in the spending of their allocated funding (ODPM, 2004c and 2004d). Whilst these are all interesting changes and proposals, they do not address the issue of *incentivising* development at the local level. Neither of the financing changes will provide additional resources to meet development pressures. Rather, they will shift the balance of resources between priorities. There is also a danger that the PGS, RIF and development tariff could reduce the amount of land coming forward for development, as they are all taxing new development. This is especially problematic within the context of government aims of increasing the overall level of housebuilding.

Huhne (2004) proposes an alternative, an annual tax on the value of land as a way of bringing forward land for development and capturing land value increases more effectively:

A tax on the value of land, or a site value rate [...] would take longer to implement [than the Barker recommendation] but would address the fundamental problem, not its symptoms. It would levy the same amount whether or not the site was used to its full potential. If the land was not developed, the landowner would have a regular charge to pay – a carry cost – that he or she does not have to pay today. He or she would therefore have an incentive either to develop or sell to someone who would develop it.

As well as incentivising development in general terms, this proposal presents the opportunity to incentivise sustainable development, by:

- encouraging the development of brownfield land;

- promoting higher densities of development;

- mitigating the costs of development in expensive areas (as, logically, more expensive areas would generate more value capture).

Additionally, if the value captured was returned to the local area this could provide local authorities with more flexibility and autonomy in meeting development needs (this point will be returned to in the next section). More work is required on the practical issues of any implementation, and any land value tax is a little way off yet. In the meantime there are also funding needs that need to be met. This said, a land value tax could well be a useful tool for delivering sustainable development, as long as any future reform recognises two fundamental factors. First, new development must be incentivised. Second, extra resources are required to meet housing needs within the South East.

Delivering development

While a land value tax may be a useful way of incentivising sustainable development, we also need to reform current governance mechanisms to deliver sustainable development. The location and type of new development across the region is critical here. Although new developments only account for a very small percentage of overall housing stock, they can have significant impacts – especially locally – and measures should be taken to mitigate this. This issue is explored further in chapters 4 and 5, water and transport respectively.

While the Barker Review's (2004) argument that at the regional level new development within the South East will only have a marginal impact on environmentally sensitive land is analytically true, it neglects the local impact of development. This is not a NIMBYist argument, although it is difficult to convince local residents of the relevance of the broader regional picture when they consider the merits or otherwise of new development. Rather, there are real challenges that need to be faced up to and addressed. A flexible approach to the greenbelt is required if we are to deliver development sustainably. For example, expanding an existing town rather than creating a new settlement is likely to be an appropriate way to deliver new housing in a way that gives better access to existing transport infrastructure.

Of course, this should be pursued within an overall policy of no net loss of greenbelt land. Local authorities should certainly also continue to apply the 'sequential approach' within the planning system – in general terms, the allocation of land for housing development must first look to appropriate brownfield land before releasing greenfield land for development – but an appropriate balance of creating new greenbelt alongside allowing some encroachment, could contribute towards delivering sustainable development. Chapter 5 considers further the need to strengthen the planning system to give greater consideration to water, sewage and flooding issues as well as discussing issues related to the type of development and more resource efficient buildings.

The density of development is often a topic that generates strong opinions on both sides of the debate. The *South East Plan: Consultation Draft* (SEERA, 2005) sets a target of 40 dwellings per hectare over the plan period. This is within the Government's density target of between 30 and 50 dwellings per hectare as promoted in Planning Policy Guidance 3 (PPG3). The South East has historically had very low densities of development (averaging around 25 dwellings per hectare) so meeting this target would represent a challenge. The *South East Plan: Consultation Draft* argues that densities have recently risen to around 30 dwellings per hectare and that 71 per cent of new development is on brownfield land (above the Government's target of 60 per cent).

Those objecting to the promotion of higher density development often point to public opinion as a reason for lower densities. It is certainly true that public opinion surveys often find that people are resistant to the development of very high density developments. Recent Joseph Rowntree Foundation research on public opinion on housing in the South East found that 79 per cent of those asked were opposed to developments of over 80 dwellings per hectare. However, this research also found that nearly half (47 per cent) of all respondents 'would like to see medium-density terraces of 45 dwellings per hectare to be built in their area and only a quarter (27 per cent) would dislike them' (Piatt et al., 2004).

Planning

There is a general recognition that there are problems around the planning regime. Debates often focus on striking an appropriate balance between allowing sufficient public consideration and democratic input into planning decisions and delivering development promptly. But the planning system itself is only one factor in the delivery of new development. The Five-Year Plan for housing (ODPM, 2005a) presents three other issues – infrastructure investment; the effective use of land, partly through excellent design; and appropriate skills (also see Egan, 2004) – as necessary to building (more) homes in England. Additionally, the Barker Review's Interim Report (2003) highlights three factors: land availability and, in particular, the complexity of developing brownfield land; the complexity of the planning process; and barriers associated with the provision of infrastructure.

Local authorities often complain that one of the biggest blocks on bringing forward new development is the lack of incentives for doing so. As the polling conducted for the *South East Plan: Consultation Draft* demonstrates, the funding of local infrastructure improvements alongside new development is often seen as a critical issue by residents (ICM, 2005). This poll also importantly showed that people did not actually 'trust' the Government to invest properly in the infrastructure to support new housing developments. Again, as discussed above, this is one of the reasons a locally collected land value tax could be useful – it could be used to fund infrastructure development alongside housing growth, especially in high cost areas.

Measures are also required to incentivise the delivery of affordable housing. The Five-Year Plan for housing suggests that a more locally-sensitive approach to delivering development will be at the heart of government strategy (ODPM, 2005a). The plan signals that local authorities are to move beyond their largely administrative role in housing policy, towards a more strategic one:

'Planning and delivering homes for the whole community needs strong leadership by local authorities. This will involve working with partners to assess the need for housing. And working in – or with – the regional assembly to develop Regional Spatial Strategies that integrate housing, economic development and new infrastructure' (ODPM, 2005a).

This seems to be an important statement in recognising that strong local leadership is key to securing the legitimacy of any housing development. It also seems a sensible approach to delivering housing needs in the South East. Local authorities should identify their housing needs – that is, the appropriate need for socially rented and intermediate housing. The infrastructure needs associated with these new developments should then be reflected in the joined-up regional authority's submissions to central government for infrastructure investment (this joined-up regional authority is discussed in more detail in chapter 4). In this way, authorities will have an incentive to bring forward development and provide affordable housing, as they will receive funding to match the scale of their commitment, also helping to improve local infrastructure.

Housing's role in regenerating less prosperous areas is also important here. Property-led regeneration in the 1980s has been shown to have often gentrified, not regenerated, less prosperous areas (Imrie and Raco, 2003). A recent joint Prime Minister's Strategy Unit and ODPM (2005) report argued that regeneration policy cannot simply focus on one factor or policy lever to regenerate less prosperous areas. Policy must recognise that these areas suffer from interlinked factors such as low levels of economic activity, poor housing and poor public services (including transport) and should therefore respond with an appropriately integrated approach to regeneration. Simply building new housing in less prosperous areas will not per se deliver regeneration.

Chapter 2 argued that a key challenge for the South East is to raise its overall employment rate, with increasing employment within less prosperous areas a significant aspect of this. Meeting this challenge could significantly help regenerate some of these areas. As an area regenerates, the housing needs and demands of the local population may change, especially if new residents move in to the area. Housing provision should respond to these changing needs and demands. Again, the local authority is best placed to identify the appropriate needs and level of demand for new housing within the local area. At all times, the aim should be to promote mixed communities. Maintaining and even extending the stock of affordable housing within a regenerated community should therefore be a central consideration.

A more flexible approach to planning periods would also be more appropriate here. The South East Plan is due to set the policy framework for housing between 2006 and 2026. However, given the limitations in housing data, including uncertainty over future international migration patterns and the increased strategic role for local authorities, setting housebuilding targets for 20 years hence does not seem sensible. Shorter planning horizons may be more appropriate, enabling more flexible and strategic responses to housing needs in the South East.

This said, there is still a need for strategic oversight at the regional level, with future scenario work an important part of this. Additionally, a Greater South East housing forum, where the regional authorities in London, the South East and East of England meet, should be established. Bramley (2005) argues that the Greater South East functions as a discreet housing market, and the evidence presented in earlier sections clearly shows the close inter-relationship between the three regions in terms of population movements. Yet there is no mechanism currently for regions to adequately reflect these inter-regional issues in their strategies. This forum should not have any powers of intervention in regional strategies. Rather, it would be up to each region to respond accordingly to the inter-regional issues presented. Importantly, however, this would be done in an open and transparent way.

Key findings

- There should be an increased provision of affordable housing in the South East. There is a clear need for both more socially rented and intermediate housing but the relative proportions of socially rented and intermediate housing should be decided at a local level. A range of different providers could deliver the extra affordable housing required in the region.

- The provision of more affordable housing within the region has public spending implications, as current government allocations are insufficient to meet the house-building targets identified in the *South East Plan: Consultation Draft*. Housing saw a sharp decline in public spending as a proportion of GDP from the early 1990s and through the first three/four years of the Labour government. More recent increases will only result in public resources for housing returning to two-thirds of the levels of national income that were being devoted in the early 1990s.

- It is not clear that significant new affordable housing will be delivered through Section 106 agreements. Indeed, much of the affordable housing delivered through Section 106 also receives some public grant. While there may be the opportunity to use a land value tax in the future to capture value uplifts and help fund infrastructure improvements, this is a number of years away and there are requirements that need to be met in the short term. Such a change to the taxation system may also be useful, however, as it will better incentivise development in local areas.

- The delivery of housing requires associated infrastructure investment to provide additional roads and public transport services, extend the capacity of water and sewerage systems, ensure adequate flood defences, and provide social and community infrastructure.

- Although the Barker Review is correct to argue that, across the region as a whole, new development will not exert significant pressure on the greenbelt and other sensitive land, this neglects local pressures from development. Changes to current governance mechanisms will also be required to deliver development sustainably.

- Local authorities should also have more of a strategic role in housing policy, so that local conditions and needs can be better reflected in development. Funding should be provided to support this development, incentivising the provision of affordable housing within mixed use communities.

- A Greater South East housing forum would also provide the opportunity to take account of inter-regional housing issues (for example, the close inter-relationship of London and the South East).

- Another significant conclusion from this analysis is that the Barker Review agenda does not seem an appropriate way of meeting housing need in the South East. This chapter has argued that this is for three reasons in particular:

  - The methodology does not seem robust, especially to set targets for 'affordability' region by region. It is unclear what increase in the supply of housing would have the desired impact on the underlying trend in house prices.

  - Bramley's (2005) modelling demonstrates that across the market cycle there will be no overall worsening of affordability in the South East, although the South East will remain England's second least affordable region.

  - To meet this affordability problem, an increase in the provision of affordable housing (both socially rented and intermediate) would be the most appropriate response.

4. Transport: keeping the South East moving

Increases in traffic congestion and pollution are cited by residents in the South East as two of their top local priorities (MORI, 2004). However, there are no signs of these quality of life pressures abating. By 2010, road traffic is expected to grow by between 23 and 29 per cent across England (DfT, 2005a) and by 25 per cent in the South East (see Table 2) compared to 2000 levels. Road transport accounts for just over a fifth of the UK's total carbon emissions (DfT, 2005a). In 2001, households in the South East had the highest levels of greenhouse gas emissions from private vehicles compared to the other English regions (ONS, 2004). The absolute and relative contribution of transport to the UK's total carbon dioxide emissions is set to increase in future years, as a consequence of further traffic growth and falling emissions in other sectors. Following a downward trend in carbon dioxide emissions since the early 1990s, in recent years emissions have started to climb again (Defra, 2005). Managing demand for road transport will be critical to cutting congestion and meeting the UK's climate change objectives.

This chapter examines how, over the longer term, a national congestion charging scheme presents the most promising option for reducing traffic congestion and pollution. It also considers how other pricing options, such as local urban charging schemes and motorway tolling, could manage traffic demand in the South East over the coming years. It recommends 'smarter' options the South East could introduce to reduce car trips and encourage greater public transport use, cycling and walking, such as travel plans and public transport marketing. It then analyses the role of planning in designing communities that prioritise the interests of pedestrians and cyclists, and the linkages between transport investment and regeneration. Finally, it makes recommendations for better co-ordinating transport policy and delivery both within the South East and across the Greater South East.

Mobility trends in the South East

Travel patterns in the South East have been broadly similar to the rest of Great Britain. Between 1992-94 and 2003, people in the South East made slightly more trips and travelled slightly longer distances, compared to their counterparts in the other English regions. The average number of trips per person per year was 1,098 in 1992-94 and 1,049 in 2003 in the South East. The average number of trips per person per year was 1,053 in 1992-94 and 990 in 2003 for Great Britain. In 2003, the average trip distance in the South East was 7.5 miles compared to the average for Great Britain of 6.9 miles – about nine per cent higher (NTS, 1992-94 to 2003).

Trip purposes in the South East have also been broadly similar to the rest of Great Britain, with the majority being for leisure purposes. Between 1985-86 and 2003, on average about 40 per cent of trips per year in the South East and in Great Britain were for leisure; with the remaining trips being equally spread over journeys for commuting and business, school and education escorts, and shopping (NTS, 1985-86 to 2003). In 2003, most people travelled to work by car – 65 per cent in the South East and 59 per cent for the Great Britain average (NTS, 2003). There is little difference in the travel-to-work times of people across Great Britain. In 2003, the average time it took for residents in the South East to travel to work was 27 minutes and the average for Great Britain was 26 minutes (NTS, 2003).

The South East is often referred to as the 'gateway' to Europe and the rest of the UK, although it is important to give this some perspective. In 2004, about two thirds of freight trips from the UK left via the South East (Dover ports or Channel Tunnel), but freight trips with a destination outside the UK only accounted for eight per cent of total freight journeys (DfT, 2004a). In 2003, about two-thirds of freight journeys beginning in the South East ended up in another part of the UK, but only ten per cent of total freight journeys within the UK had their origin in the South East (DfT, 2003). Moving more freight journeys from road to rail would help to reduce their contribution to overall road congestion.

In 2003, freight traffic accounted for about five per cent of all road traffic in the South East with the highest proportion coming from private vehicles (DfT, 2004b). Between 1996 and 2003, the South East had the highest proportion of households with two cars and the lowest proportion of households with no car, compared to the other English regions (NTS, 1996 and 2003). Figure 1 shows that in 2003, motorists in the South East drove more miles by car compared to most other English regions (NTS, 2003). These high levels of car ownership and use reflect the relative affluence of the region.

Figure 1: Average distance by car per year by English region, 2003

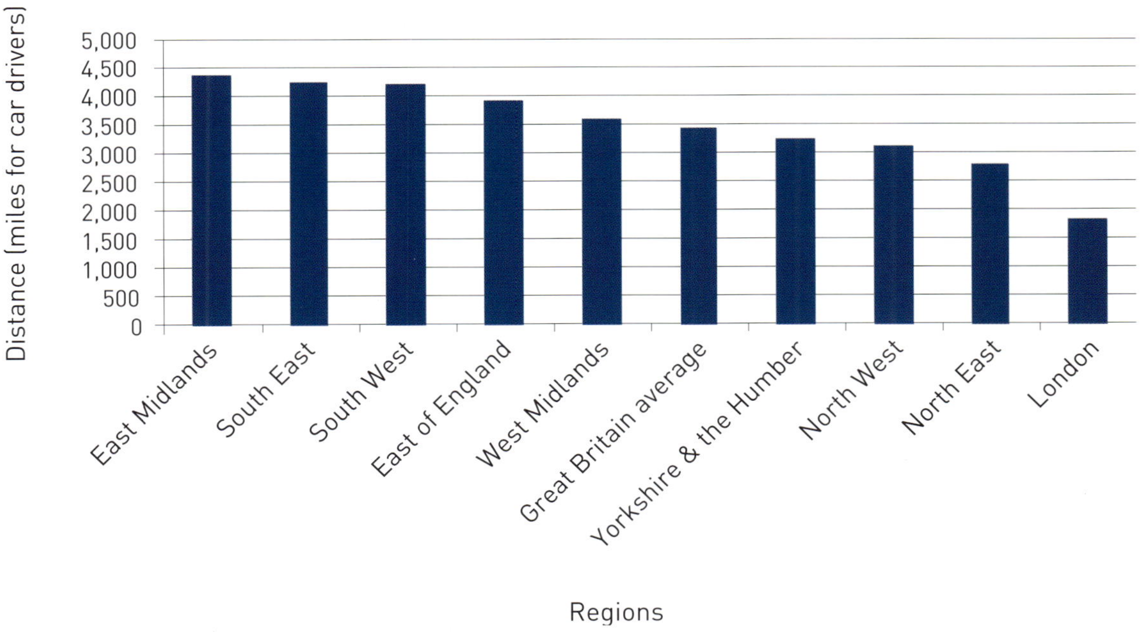

Source: NTS, 2003

Figure 2 shows that in 2001, greenhouse gas emissions from private vehicles per household in the South East were 3.2 tonnes of carbon dioxide equivalent compared to the UK average of 2.6 tonnes of carbon dioxide equivalent (ONS, 2004).

Figure 2: Greenhouse gas emissions per household by English region from private vehicles, 2001

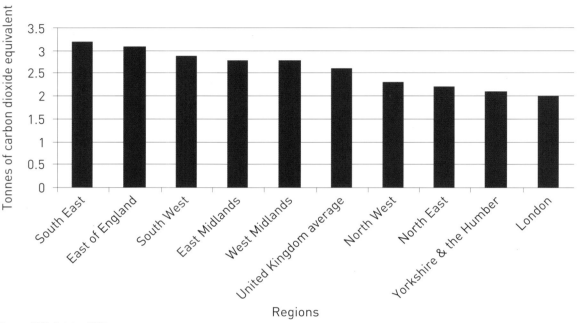

Source: ONS, October 2004

It is often asserted that the UK has some of the highest levels of traffic congestion compared to other European countries. However, information on the comparison of delays caused by congestion is fairly out of date. One of the most referenced sources is a 1996 study by the European Centre for Infrastructure Studies which showed that almost a quarter of the most well used links in the UK suffered delays lasting an hour or more whilst such delays occurred on less than one in ten links in Germany and France. Several countries had no links at all with delays of an hour or more (ECIS, 1996 cited in CfIT, 2001). More recent data, however, suggests this may give a distorted view of people's actual travel experiences. Figure 3 suggests that commuting times for journeys to work in the UK have been fairly similar to other European countries – in 2000 the UK had a similar proportion of commuting trips under 20 minutes and 30 minutes compared to the EU average (for the 15 member states).

A legacy of under-spending on transport

The UK's transport system has suffered from years of under-spending from successive governments. Figure 4 shows that from 1993-94 to 1999-00 public spending on transport was squeezed and the increase in spending from 1999-00 served only to bring spending in 2004-05, as a percentage of GDP, back up to the level it was in 1995-96.

Figure 3: Commuting times across a range of European countries, 2000

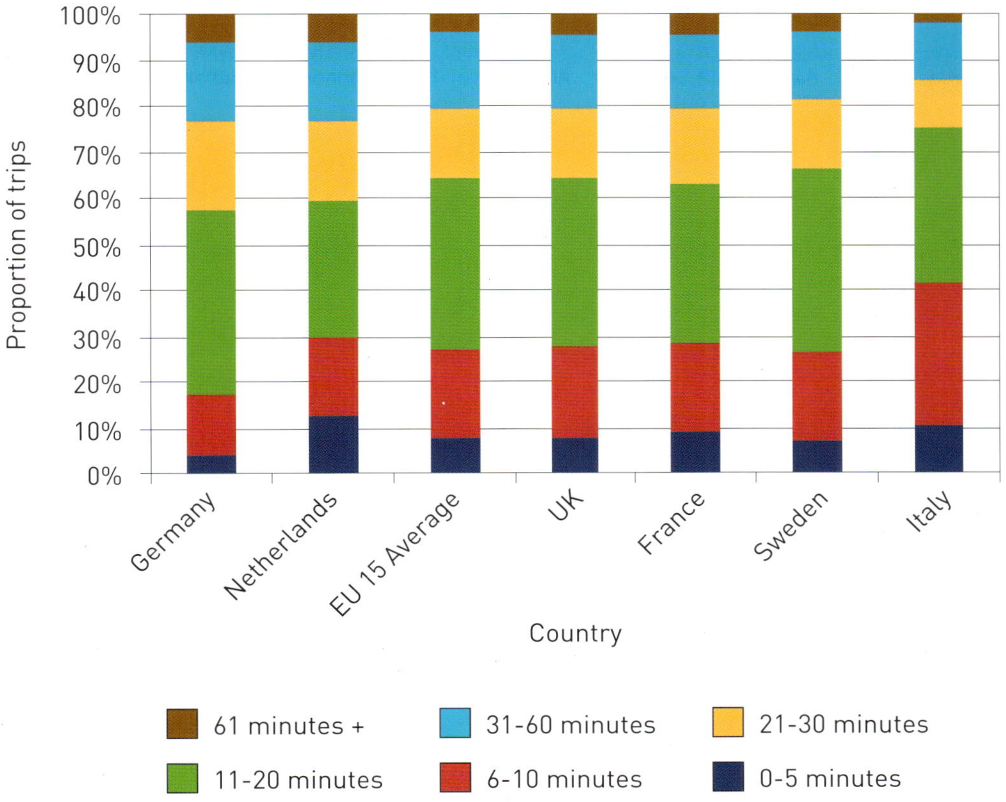

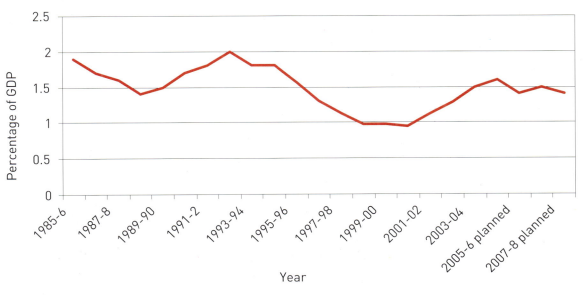

Y-axis: Proportion of trips (0% to 100%)

X-axis (Country): Germany, Netherlands, EU 15 Average, UK, France, Sweden, Italy

Legend:
- 61 minutes +
- 31-60 minutes
- 21-30 minutes
- 11-20 minutes
- 6-10 minutes
- 0-5 minutes

Source: European Foundation, Working Conditions Survey, 2000

Figure 4: Public spending on transport in the UK as a percentage of GDP from 1985-86 to 2007-08

Y-axis: Percentage of GDP (0 to 2.5)

X-axis (Year): 1985-6, 1987-8, 1989-90, 1991-2, 1993-94, 1995-96, 1997-98, 1999-00, 2001-02, 2003-04, 2005-6 planned, 2007-8 planned

Source: Public Expenditure Statistical Analyses, HM Treasury, 2005a and HMTreasury, 2004a

Figure 5 shows the South East's share of public spending on transport. Between 1998-99 and 2004-05 the South East has received transport funding comparable to the other English regions and UK nations. London stands out as having received a significantly higher level of transport expenditure per capita.

Figure 5: Average expenditure on transport per region between 1998-99 to 2004-05

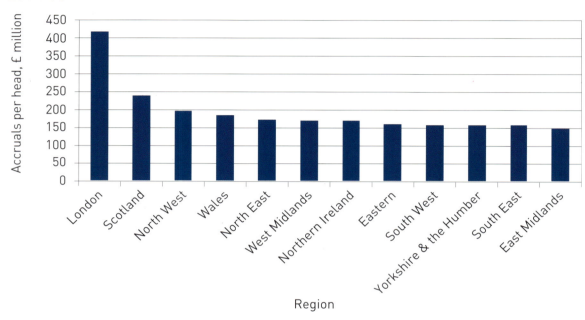

Source: Public Expenditure Statistical Analyses, HM Treasury, 2005a

Information comparing public investment in transport infrastructure across EU countries is either patchy or out of date. Figure 6 shows the latest comparative data for government investment in all public infrastructure across a selected range of EU countries. This includes transport infrastructure spending. Since the 1980s, the UK has had one of the lowest levels of government investment in infrastructure compared to most other EU countries. Over the period 1996 to 2002, infrastructure spending in the UK was lower than the EU average at 1.3 per cent of GDP compared to 2.2 per cent of GDP for the EU-15 average (EC, 2004).

Over the next parliamentary term, central government spending on transport is likely to remain limited as health, education and international development have been prioritised as the top spending areas. Transport spending, as a percentage of GDP, was broadly stabilised in the 2004 Spending Review. The Government expects public spending on transport to level off at 1.4 per cent of GDP by 2007-08 (HMT, 2004a). This is below the levels of the 1980s and well below the last years of the Major government. A recent Government consultation on regional funding allocations acknowledged that 'due to current cost pressures on rail, the Government is not planning a major capital programme of rail enhancements – of a kind comparable to local authority and Highways Agency major scheme expenditure – in the near future' (HMT/DfT/ODPM/DTI, 2004).

Figure 6: Government gross fixed capital formation across a selection of EU countries between 1980 and 2002

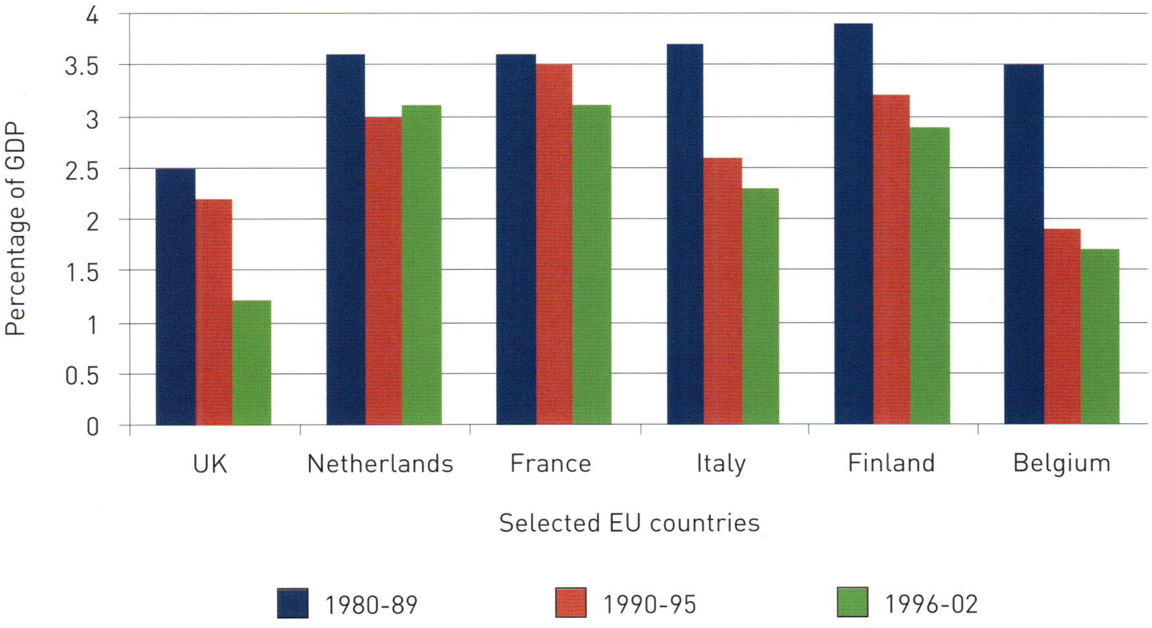

Source: EC, 2004

The additional transport infrastructure costs of the South East growth areas

The South East, as with every other region, will find it increasingly difficult to find the resources necessary to fund additional transport improvements. This could pose a challenge to the delivery of the Government's Sustainable Communities Plan (ODPM, 2003). The 2004 Spending Review announced a £200 million CIF to support transport investment to enable faster housing development in the growth areas, including those in the South East (HMT, 2004a). Bids totalling £600 million were received and these were whittled down to £225 million, based on their deliverability (the CIF can only be paid in 2006/7 and 2007/8) and the contribution they would make to housing growth. Table 1 shows the bids being taken forward for appraisal across the growth areas in the Greater South East. About 40 per cent of the bids are for the growth areas in the South East including Milton Keynes and Ashford, as well as the South East parts of the Thames Gateway.

It is difficult to make an assessment of the additional transport infrastructure costs associated with new housing developments. The South East growth areas are dispersed throughout the region and the two largest growth areas are in the established urban centres of Milton Keynes and Ashford. The issue for these growth areas will be the additional costs of extending the capacity of existing transport infrastructure, or improving existing transport services.

The CIF is unlikely to be sufficient to meet the future additional transport infrastructure costs associated with the growth areas, particularly bearing in mind that the housing growth proposals in the Sustainable Communities Plan look out to 2016 and

2031. The Budget 2005 announced that the Government had commissioned Rod Eddington, former Chief Executive of British Airways, to report on Britain's long term transport needs (HMT, 2005b), which may shed further light on the future transport infrastructure costs of the South East and its planned growth areas.

Table 1: The distribution and types of bids to the Community Infrastructure Fund

Growth Area	Authority	Amount (£m)	Examples of the types of projects
Thames Gateway	Essex	17.7	Platform lengthening on the Barking-Dagenham-Grays-Pitsea rail route in Essex which will open the way for longer trains serving this route; the Rushenden Relief Road on the Isle of Sheppey in Kent; and transport improvements to Woolwich town.
	Kent	29.3	
	London	20.4	
	Total	67.4	
Milton Keynes-South Midlands	Milton Keynes	32.4	A new railway station to serve planned developments in Berryfields in Aylesbury; upgrading of Junction 14 and the M1 and an upgrade of Milton Keynes Central Station; and construction of a four-platform station to support the new community at Wixams, South Bedford.
	Aylesbury, Bucks	19.4	
	Northamptonshire	33.7	
	Luton UA	21.7	
	Bedfordshire	3.9	
	Total	111.1	
London-Stansted-Peterborough	London	18	Widening Fletton Parkway to support further expansion to the new community at the Hamptons in Peterborough; a new spine road for Haringey Heartlands; and transport improvements in Ilford Town Centre to ease congestion.
	Peterborough	7	
	Essex	5.8	
	Herts	6.6	
	Cambridgeshire	1.6	
	Total	39	
Ashford	Kent	7.7	Remodelling Ashford's ring road to help regenerate the central area.
	Total	7.7	
CIF total		**225.2**	

Source: Table assembled from information in a DfT press release, 17th March 2005b

Note: The total value of the schemes being considered exceeds the £200 million budget of the CIF and so some schemes may not be fully funded from the CIF.

Funding transport improvements in the South East

There are two options for raising additional revenue for paying for much needed public transport improvements in the South East. The first is from increased spending from government through taxation. The second is from user charges. The chapter on housing discussed alternative mechanisms for raising revenue such as land value taxation and Section 106 agreements. This chapter will focus on the role for road user charging.

There is a growing recognition amongst politicians and the public that we cannot build our way out of our transport problems. The UK, and congested regions like the South East, are facing a tough choice between increasing traffic delays and pollution or bold measures for managing traffic growth and reducing car dependency. There is no doubt that road transport provides people and businesses with convenience and flexibility. Road user charging is often accused of being 'anti-motorist.' In fact, it is about developing a fairer way of paying for road use that accounts for the external costs motoring imposes on society through congestion and pollution.

The success of the Central London congestion charge has undoubtedly helped to build political momentum for the use of price signals in reducing demand for road transport. Traffic levels have been cut by 15 per cent and congestion by 30 per cent in the charging zone. Of the 65,000 to 70,000 fewer car trips made into Central London, between 50 and 60 per cent have been transferred to public transport (TfL, 2004). Alongside 'The Future of Transport' White Paper (DfT, 2004c) which sets out transport policies looking out to 2015, the Government published a Road Pricing Feasibility Study (DfT, 2004d) on options for introducing a national road pricing scheme. The White Paper states that 'the Government view is that the costs of inaction and unrestricted road building are too high for society. The time has come to seriously consider the role that could be played by some form of road pricing policy' (DfT, 2004c).

The principal purpose of congestion charging is to reduce journey times and traffic jams in some of the busiest hot spots. However, congestion charging could also potentially raise extra resources to pay for future transport improvements. A national congestion charging scheme could potentially raise in the region of £16 billion per year (in 2010 prices) of which £2.5 billion per year (in 2010 prices) would be from the South East (excluding any operating costs). But it is important to acknowledge that a national, comprehensive congestion charging scheme is unlikely to be something any government could implement any time soon. It could take at least ten years before it is technically feasible at a viable cost.

It will be difficult to win public support for an eventual, national congestion charging scheme unless there is increased spending on transport to offer accessible, reliable and cost-effective transport options. Survey evidence suggests that motorists would find road user charging acceptable if it were part of a package of better roads, public transport and traffic management (RAC Foundation, 2002). This, in effect, is what Ken Livingstone, the Mayor of London, did when the Central London congestion charge was introduced. In conjunction with the scheme, the Mayor committed to additional spending of £84 million on bus services to ensure that people travelling around central London would have an accessible and reliable alternative to the car.

If politicians are to win public support for national congestion charging, in the years preceding the introduction of the scheme there will need to be increased public spending on transport, to offer accessible, reliable and cost-effective transport options. But this presents a funding conundrum – while a national congestion charging scheme could potentially raise additional revenue to pay for transport improvements, it will not do so for at least another decade. Bearing in mind public spending on transport will be limited over the next parliamentary term, the Government is faced with the problem of how it can start to invest in transport improvements over the short to medium term to make the longer term introduction of a national congestion charging scheme publicly palatable.

One option is to increase transport investment by financing it through extra government borrowing. This would not have consequences for the Treasury's 'golden rule' which allows for borrowing to finance investment. It would, however, increase the debt-GDP ratio and therefore the future burden of interest payments to be borne by the taxpayer. These interest payments could be met by some of the future revenues raised from a national congestion charging scheme. This option could increase the pressure on any future government to introduce a national congestion charging scheme. However, without making a commitment to improve transport options and introduce national congestion charging over the longer term, we will simply be passing on the problems of rising congestion to future generations to solve.

A new way of paying for road use – road user charging

Nationally, there is a perception that motorists already pay a high rate of tax in the UK, in the case of fuel tax much higher than in other European countries. But these perceptions do not take account of other taxes such as road tolls and vehicle purchase taxes. In fact, UK drivers are not the most heavily taxed in Europe – that accolade belongs to motorists in the Netherlands – and they pay similar levels of tax overall to drivers in France, Italy, Ireland, Finland and Denmark (CfIT, 2001). It is also not widely appreciated that, over the last twenty years, the costs of motoring have been falling, largely due to improvements in vehicle efficiency, whilst the costs of public transport have been rising. Even in the short period between 1997 and 2003, the costs of motoring fell by 4.8 per cent (Parliamentary Answer, Tony McNulty MP, 2004). Between 1980 and 2003-04, average rail fares rose by 40 per cent and average bus fares outside of London rose by 46 per cent in real terms (DfT, 2004e).

There is long established evidence that people value the savings they get from reducing the amount of time spent travelling. According to the CBI, congestion and poor quality transport can affect the investment decisions of businesses (CBI, 2004). The Road Pricing Feasibility Study (DfT, 2004d) estimated that a national road user charging scheme could achieve as much as £12 billion worth of time savings a year – in 1998 prices. Road user charging could therefore reduce the costs incurred by individuals, industry and commerce in the South East through delays and unreliable journeys.

There are broadly three types of road user charging schemes. Firstly, payment for entering a specific area such as the Central London congestion charge. Secondly, payment for using a new road such as the M6 Toll in Birmingham, which opened in December 2003. Thirdly, payment for using existing road capacity, as with the German lorry road user charge that was introduced in 2004. The Government plans to introduce a similar scheme for Heavy Goods Vehicles (HGVs) in the UK by 2007-08 with pilots in 2006 (HMT/HM C&E/DfT, 2005).

Longer term option: a national congestion charging scheme

The Government is currently considering options for moving towards a national congestion charging scheme over the longer term. National congestion charging would move away from the current system of motoring taxation, towards a fairer way of paying for road use based on congestion levels. Motorists who drive on the most congested roads at peak times would, therefore, be charged more than motorists who use less busy roads at off peak times. It is likely that a national scheme would require a 'black box' on board the vehicle which could work out exactly where, when and over what distance the vehicle is being driven, possibly using a satellite positioning system (DfT, 2004c).

Professor Stephen Glaister and Dr Dan Graham of Imperial College were commissioned to explore the potential effects national congestion charging could have if it were introduced on all roads throughout England in 2010. The scheme would affect all vehicles. The assumptions used in this modelling are shown in the appendix. Two charging scenarios for congestion charging in 2010 were tested: 1. revenue raising – where congestion charges are added to existing motoring costs and 2. revenue neutral – where congestion charges are offset by cuts in fuel tax so that no net extra revenue is raised.

Table 2: Traffic change between 2000 and 2010 for various charging scenarios (compared to a 'business as usual' scenario in 2000)

	South East	England average
'Business as usual'	+25%	+27%
Revenue neutral charging scheme	+34%	+35%
Revenue raising charging scheme	+16%	+18%

Source: Modelling by Imperial College commissioned by ippr

Table 2 shows that, assuming 'business as usual' conditions, traffic is likely to rise steeply in the South East by 25 per cent by 2010 (from a base year of 2000). Under the revenue neutral charging scheme, traffic could rise at an even higher rate of 34 per cent in the South East and 35 per cent across England. Revenue neutral congestion charging would see a growth in overall traffic levels, particularly in rural areas, which would be undesirable for quality of life in the countryside. In addition, the cost of motoring is expected to fall by around 30 per cent over the period to 2010, due to a combination of reductions in the real fuel price and fuel efficiency improvements (DfT, 2005a). The increase in rural traffic compounded by falling motoring costs explains why a revenue neutral charge leads to the perverse result of an overall increase in the rate of traffic growth. While it may be politically easier to introduce congestion charging on a revenue neutral basis with offsetting fuel duty reductions, this approach would not have the desired impact on traffic growth. Other studies on congestion charging options have come to the same conclusion (e.g. Ekins and Dresner, 2004).

Introducing congestion charging on a revenue raising basis, whereby charges are added on top of fuel duty costs, would not reverse the upward trend in traffic levels. But it would help to reduce the *rate* at which traffic is set to grow. Under a revenue raising scheme, traffic would increase at a lower rate of 16 per cent in the South East. Even under a revenue raising charging scheme, policy-makers would also need to employ other measures for reducing traffic growth. Figure 7 shows that the South East would benefit from average traffic reductions under a national congestion charging scheme that was revenue raising in 2010. London would benefit from the largest reductions in traffic under any scheme.

Figure 7: Percentage change in road traffic resulting from congestion charging across the English regions in 2010 (compared to a 'business as usual scenario' in 2000).

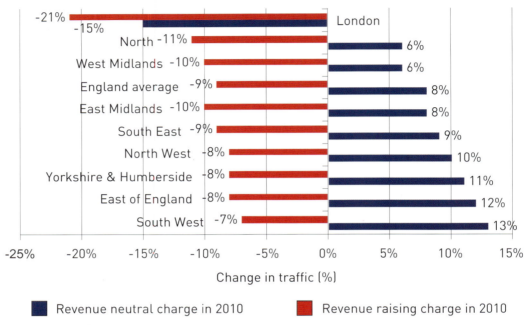

Change in traffic (%)

■ Revenue neutral charge in 2010   ■ Revenue raising charge in 2010

Source: Modelling by Imperial College commissioned by ippr

The modelling results found a revenue neutral charge could lead to a five per cent *increase* in carbon dioxide emissions by 2010 across England while a revenue raising charge could *reduce* carbon dioxide emissions by about eight per cent by 2010 across England. Carbon dioxide emissions from new cars are expected to fall by 25 per cent by 2008, as a result of a European voluntary agreement with car manufacturers. But the growth in traffic is projected to cancel out these improvements. Designing a national charging scheme that is revenue raising will therefore also be important to curbing road transport's contribution to climate change.

A House of Commons Transport Select Committee report found that even those businesses that preferred a revenue neutral approach to congestion charging, viewed this in broad terms (HoC Transport Select Committee, 2005). Business representatives suggested to the Transport Committee that revenue neutrality could not only be achieved with lower taxes, but also by improving transport services which would benefit the motorist.

The revenue raised from congestion charging

If a revenue raising charge were introduced across England in 2010 it could potentially raise £16 billion per year in 2010 prices. This is about £14 billion per year in 2004-05 prices. Figure 8 shows the revenue results disaggregated by English region. The highest charges would be paid by motorists in the Greater South East including London and the South East. A national congestion charging scheme could potentially raise £2.5 billion per year (in 2010 prices) in the South East. This is about £2.2 billion per year in 2004-05 prices.

Figure 8: The additional revenue raised from a congestion charge introduced in 2010 in the English regions (2010 prices)

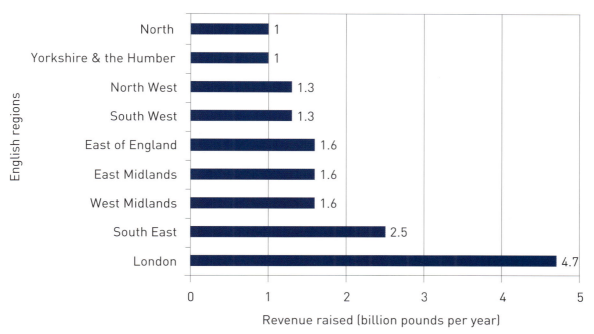

Source: Modelling by Imperial College commissioned by ippr.

The results for the revenue raised from congestion charging need to be treated with caution as they are just an illustration of what could potentially be raised and not definitive amounts. Also, they do not account for the costs that would be incurred from setting up and administering a national scheme which could be significant. It is very difficult to predict the costs of future congestion charge technologies, but it has been estimated that the technology needed to set up a national scheme could cost in the region of £3 billion. The further costs of administering and enforcing the scheme have been estimated at between £2 billion and £3 billion per year (DfT, 2004d).

If part of the public deal for persuading motorists to accept a national congestion charging scheme is to bring forward transport investment, then part of the revenue may be needed to service the extra debt taken on by the Government to finance that upfront investment. At the same time, there is considerable political support for the idea that some of the future revenue raised from motorists should be redistributed back to the regions and that local people should have a say about how that money is spent locally. In the South East, there is support for the idea that the revenue raised from motorists travelling in the South East should be earmarked for transport improvements that benefit the people of the South East.

There is, however, a trade-off between using the revenue gains from a national congestion charging scheme to fund upfront transport investment initially financed through borrowing, and using the revenue to pay for transport improvements in future decades. A balance will need to be struck between the two. The RAC Foundation has argued that an independent body, rather than HM Treasury, should be set up to distribute the revenue raised, to provide the public with reassurance that they will see the benefits of any money raised and that it will be used to fund transport improvements and not other future public policy priorities (RAC Foundation, 2002).

Fairness for motorists in the South East

Of the revenue raised from motorists in the South East, over a third would be paid by motorists in rural areas, which is a higher proportion than the other English regions. Within the South East, more than two million people live in small rural villages and the countryside and nearly a quarter of all South East businesses are based in rural areas (SEEDA, 2002). An important political concern is the impact congestion charging could have on businesses and low income households in rural areas of the South East. Low income households, particularly those in rural areas, can spend up to a quarter of their disposable income running a car and would find it difficult to manage without one (DfT, 2004c).

Table 3 shows the effects of congestion charging on the operating costs (non-fuel and fuel operating costs) of motorists in rural and urban areas in 2010. It compares the average operating costs per kilometre and per mile across the English regions and for the South East region. In the South East, the operating costs per kilometre could be 10.8 pence for a rural motorist and 16.4 pence for an urban motorist with a congestion charge, compared to 9.4 pence and 11.1 pence respectively without a congestion charge. Rural motorists in the South East might therefore pay, on average, just over one penny more per kilometre or just over two pence more per mile, after the introduction of a charge. A revenue raising charge would not significantly increase the operating costs of motoring in rural areas of the South East, where there can be few public transport alternatives to the car. It would, however, significantly increase the operating costs and thus help to reduce the demand for urban driving in the South East.

Table 3: Average operating costs for rural versus urban motorists (travelling by car) in 2010

| | Average operating costs (pence per kilometre and mile) | | | |
| | Rural (population <10,000) | | Urban (population between 25,000 and 250,000) | |
	England average	South East	England average	South East
No charge	9.6p/km 15.4p/mile	9.4p/km 15p/mile	11.1p/km 17.8p/mile	11.1p 17.8p/mile
Revenue raising charge	10.7p/km 17.1p/mile	10.8p/km 17.3p/mile	15.7p/km 25.1p/mile	16.4p/km 26.2p/mile

Source: Modelling by Imperial College commissioned by ippr

Notes: The money cost includes the non-fuel operating costs (road charges, maintenance and insurance) and fuel operating costs (including fuel duty). It is based on a weighted average cost for all types of road and for all times of the day.

As a fixed cost, Vehicle Excise Duty (VED) hits low income, low mileage motorists the hardest, while providing no incentive for high income, high mileage motorists to drive less. As a consequence, various independent studies have recommended that a further way in which the Government could win over public support for a revenue raising national congestion charging scheme would be to reduce or abolish VED (Ekins and Dresner, 2004; Grayling et al., 2004).

Short to medium term pathways: lorry road user charge, motorway tolling, local urban charging schemes and congestion busting lanes

The Government's view is that it could take at least ten years before it is technically feasible to introduce a national congestion charging scheme (DfT, 2004c). Uncertainties relating to the kinds of technologies needed for administering and enforcing a national scheme would need to be resolved. Many European countries favour the use of Global Positioning Satellite (GPS) tracking technology which can pinpoint a vehicle's location on any road at any time of the day. There have, however, been concerns that using such technology could be an infringement on people's civil liberties. All this points to the need for the Government to start developing a congestion charging strategy as early as possible so that it can engage the public in a debate about how a national scheme might work. In the meantime, there are short to medium term pathways that policy-makers in the Government and the South East can employ to reduce traffic growth while helping to build the case for a national congestion charging scheme.

Lorry road user charge

The Government is preparing to introduce a distance based charging scheme for lorries in 2007-08 and has been consulting on the scheme (HMT/HM C&E/DfT, 2005). The scheme will apply to all HGVs driving on UK roads with a plated weight of 3.5 tonnes or more, including those registered abroad. Unlike a congestion charge, the lorry road user charge will be based on mileage rather than levels of congestion. The second progress report for the proposed introduction of the HGV scheme recognised that 'satellite-based systems probably offer the best way forward, since they have the most flexibility for charging all roads' (HMT, 2003). The lorry road user charge will enable a trial run of the technology that could be used for implementing a future national scheme for cars.

The Government has announced that the lorry road user charge will be revenue neutral, with lorry drivers being able to claim a rebate on part of the duty paid on fuel, so that the UK haulage industry will not have to pay any more tax overall (HMT, 2004b). But our modelling results suggest that a lorry user charge that is designed to be revenue neutral could either have no impact on traffic levels or, at worst, lead to a slight increase in traffic. A future lorry road user charge will only help to ease congestion on major motorway routes and reduce the journey times of individuals and businesses in the South East and elsewhere, if it is designed to be revenue raising.

Motorway tolling on congested commuter routes as well as tolling on major motorway sections that are due to be widened

The technologies for enforcing tolling have been proven across Europe. The M6 Toll Road in Birmingham was built to provide an alternative to the M6, which is one of the busiest motorway routes in Britain. On the M6 Toll Road the majority of drivers pay cash into a collecting bucket as they pass the toll booth, although it is also possible to pay electronically using a microwave tag system. Tolling could also be introduced on major motorway routes that are due to be widened, such as sections of the M25 that run through parts of the South East. The Road Pricing Feasibility Study estimated that the cost of establishing tolled lanes on the 435 kilometres of the strategic road network classified as 'severely congested' could be about £643 million and that the annual running costs would be in the order of £250 million (DfT, 2004d).

The M6 Toll Road was privately financed and is operated by a private company. The contract period is for the next 50 years and the revenue is collected by the private operators running the road. It therefore generates no additional funding that can be used for transport projects that have a wider public benefit. The M6 Toll contract was criticised by the House of Commons Transport Select Committee for handing too much control to the private sector, which has the power to set the levels of charges on the toll road. It argued that this kind of contractual arrangement compromised the ability of the Government and the Highways Agency (responsible for strategic road networks outside of London) to manage traffic policies across the UK (HoC Transport Select Committee, 2005). For instance, it is unclear how the operation of the M6 Toll will coordinate with the planned lorry road user charge and any charges that are set for HGVs on other parts of the strategic road network. Government policies can be applied to the M6 Toll Road with the co-operation of the operators and there is no guarantee this will work in the public interest.

A more preferable option is to introduce motorway tolling as part of a public-private partnership. A private company could administer the scheme, with the revenue being shared between the public and private sector. This would ensure that the Government and the Highways Agency are still able to regulate the level of charges and that some of the revenue is available for funding transport improvements. In cases where motorway routes need to be widened, or where a new motorway needs to be built, a public-private partnership could help to reduce the financial risks of investing in new road capacity.

In recent years there have been significant technical advances in cleaner fuels and technologies for vehicles that produce less pollution (DfT, 2001). For instance, hybrid-electric vehicles that combine an electric battery with an engine, offer fuel efficiency improvements over conventional vehicles of 30-50 per cent (Foley, 2003). Hybrid-electric vehicles are already supplied by several leading vehicle manufacturers and benefit from a government purchase grant. The Government currently provides purchase grants and some tax incentives for cleaner vehicles. But these tax incentives will need to be significantly increased if the Government is to encourage greater take up of cleaner vehicles. Exempting cleaner vehicles from future motorway tolls would help to encourage more motorists, particularly company car drivers, to choose low polluting vehicles.

Local urban charging schemes

Local authorities already have the powers under the Transport Act 2000 to introduce urban charging schemes – subject to the approval of the Secretary of State for Transport. There is limited scope for introducing an urban area based charging scheme on the scale of the London congestion charge, owing to an absence of a large metropolitan area in the South East. However, the Multi-Modal Study for the South East Corridor recommended a role for smaller-scale urban congestion charging in Brighton and Southampton-Portsmouth (GOSE, 2002). Quality of life surveys reveal that residents in Southampton have some of the highest concerns about traffic congestion and air pollution (Foley, 2004). The *South East Plan: Consultation Draft* (SEERA, 2005) calls on local authorities to make appropriate use of their powers to introduce congestion charging schemes in some of the South East's busiest urban centres.

It is important to recognise that although many, including the Government, view local urban charging schemes as an effective tool for tackling congestion in the short term and as a useful step towards a national scheme, some local authorities and local people still have serious reservations (HoC, 2005). This was illustrated by the three to one rejection of the city-wide congestion charging proposal in Edinburgh. Ultimately it is up to local communities and not central government to decide whether an urban charging scheme is the best way to manage traffic demand in a local area.

If the Government wants to see local urban charging being progressed, it will need to provide local authorities with incentives to encourage them to win public support locally. The Government is already starting to do this through the Transport Innovation Fund (TIF) which rises to £2.5 billion per year by 2015. The idea is that local authorities can bid for funds to support radical plans for managing traffic, such as congestion charging. Alongside this, local authorities may also gain greater control over bus services through quality contracts which regulate routes, fares and timetables (DfT, 2004c). The question is whether the TIF will be sufficient. The TIF could be broken down into regional funding pots, leaving it up to local authorities and regional bodies to decide what traffic demand projects should take priority for funding.

As with the London congestion charge, vehicles running on cleaner fuels and technologies should be exempted from local urban charging schemes. Hybrid-electric vehicles offer a particular air quality advantage in busy urban areas, because in stop-start driving conditions they run on their zero emission battery.

Car pooling lanes

There appears to be growing Government interest in the role for car pooling lanes – dedicated lanes for vehicles carrying two or more people. In December 2004, it was announced that the first High Occupancy Vehicle (HOV) motorway lane will be trialled on the M1 between junctions 7 and 10 (Milton Keynes South to St Albans) by 2008 (DfT, 2004f). In March 2005, it was also announced that the Highways Agency will be examining whether a car pooling lane could be introduced on the M25 between junctions 12 and 15 (M3-M4) (DfT, 2005c). Car pooling lanes are already used alongside highways in the United States to encourage drivers to share cars and reduce congestion. There is a strong case for exploring options for further car pooling lanes, especially along the busiest motorway routes between the South East and London to help reduce congestion at peak commuter times.

Smarter travel choices – encouraging public transport use, cycling and walking

The 2004 report 'Smarter Choices: Changing the Way We Travel', published by the DfT, highlighted the role that smarter travel measures could play in helping to cut congestion, while encouraging public transport use, cycling or walking. Options such as personalised travel planning, public transport marketing, travel plans and car clubs focus on improving information about travel choices, rather than altering the regulatory or charging framework within which travel choices are made. However, experience suggests that they tend to be most effective when combined with harder-edged, demand management measures. Road user charging and smarter travel measures should therefore be viewed by policy-makers as part of a package of complementary measures needed for reducing car trips. Compared to investing in new road infrastructure projects, smarter travel measures have the advantage that they can be put into effect much more quickly and cost effectively.

The application of smarter travel measures in the UK has been fairly small scale, although there is considerable potential for scaling up their implementation, particularly in urban areas where there is likely to be greater access to public transport alternatives to the car. The Smarter Choices report (DfT, 2004g) found that scaling up a combination of smarter travel measures could reduce urban traffic, in peak hours, by as much as 21 per cent across the UK. Given a revenue raising national congestion charge could only reduce the rate at which traffic is set to increase (it could reduce the rate of traffic growth in the South East by about nine per cent by 2010) the potential for smarter travel measures cannot be neglected. Policy-makers in the South East should be taking them forward at a larger scale without delay.

Travel plans

Travel plans offer one of the most promising smarter options for reducing car trips in the South East. A workplace travel plan is a package of measures put in place by an employer to try and encourage more sustainable travel – usually meaning less car use or less single occupancy car use (DfT, 2004g). Typical measures include communication and marketing measures, car pooling, cycle leasing, and the provision of company buses. Given 74 per cent of residents in the South East travelled to work by car in 2003 (NTS, 2003), work travel plans could help to reduce congestion during peak travel-to-work times. The Smarter Choices report suggested that, by 2013-14, work travel plans could potentially cover 50 per cent of the working population in urban areas across the UK and could reduce car trips by nine per cent during peak travel times. The cost of each car kilometre reduced by work travel plans could be as low as between 0.1 and two pence (DfT, 2004g). The South East could achieve similar levels of coverage, if best practice work travel plans were rolled across the region over the next ten years.

School travel plans operate in a similar manner to workplace travel plans with the onus placed on schools to develop safe and sustainable travel to school. Plans include parentally supervised 'walking buses' and 'cycle trains' as well as bus use promotion through discounted ticketing and dedicated school buses. The Government has a target for every school in England to have a travel plan by 2010 (DfT, 2004c). The Smarter Choices report forecast that this could result in a 20 per cent reduction in school escort car trips during the peak morning and off-peak afternoon periods (DfT, 2004g). The cost of each car kilometre reduced by school travel plans could range from 1.4 to ten pence, depending on take-up of the scheme (DfT, 2004g). This is indicative of the potential scale of effect at the regional level in the South East. Buckinghamshire County Council has been leading the development of school travel plans and predicts that 80 per cent of its schools will be engaged in travel plans by 2006. For the schools participating in travel plans in Buckinghamshire, car journeys fell from 45 per cent to 37 per cent between 2002 and 2003 (Buckinghamshire County Council, 2003).

The majority of trips in the South East and across Great Britain are for leisure purposes (NTS, 1985-86 to 2003). Unlike school and work travel, leisure travel takes place at different times throughout the day and to geographically dispersed destinations, which makes it more difficult to reduce car trips for leisure purposes. Options include designing travel plans for specific sites, such as sports centres, or using public transport marketing to raise awareness of bus services to and from leisure destinations. For instance, as part of Brighton and Hove City Council's 'Breeze up to the Downs' initiative, it has been publicising the bus routes it runs from the city to popular countryside locations (Brighton and Hove City Council, 2005).

Personalised travel planning

Personalised travel planning involves the use of direct techniques for providing information to individuals or households, aimed at encouraging them to choose a different pattern of travel behaviour. The information provided is personalised to suit individual travel needs. Incentives such as free or discounted tickets for public transport services, are also offered. Personalised travel planning tends to focus on journeys for which a modal switch is easily possible. In 2002-03, 22 per cent of car trips per person in the South East were less than two miles (NTS, 2002-03). Many of these shorter car trips could feasibly be made by foot, bike or bus.

The largest applications of personalised travel planning so far have been in Western Australia. In the UK there have been small scale projects in Bristol, Gloucester, Nottingham and Sheffield, and the DfT are funding further projects. The initial pilots in Gloucester and Frome during 2001-02 reduced car driver trips by nine per cent and six per cent respectively and both led to increases in walking and cycling (Sustrans, 2004). For the Frome pilot, the total budget for the 500 people targeted was £72,000 implying an average cost of £144 per person (Sustrans, 2002). Transport for London (TfL) has estimated that a larger scale scheme, targeting 120,000 to 150,000 Londoners, could cost £1.3 million, implying an average cost of about £10 per person (in DfT, 2004g). The Smarter Choices report suggested that, by 2013-14, the large scale application of personalised travel planning could potentially reduce car trips in urban areas across the UK by up to five per cent (DfT, 2004g), although personalised travel planning is generally more costly than travel plans.

Public transport marketing

Public transport marketing tends to be employed in combination with demand management measures, or financial incentives for increasing patronage of local public transport services. In the UK, bus service improvements have tended to take the form of a public-private partnership – called a quality bus partnership – whereby local authorities and bus operators work together and share the costs of improving local bus services and undertaking promotional activity. In the South East, if more local authorities were to combine public transport marketing with improvements in local bus services, they could significantly increase bus patronage in both urban and rural areas.

> ### Brighton and Hove bus service improvements
> Public transport information and marketing in Brighton and Hove is a mixture of closely related hard and soft initiatives. In 1998, Brighton and Hove City Council entered into a quality bus partnership with Brighton and Hove Bus Company and since then the bus network has undergone fundamental changes. Brighton and Hove Bus Company has rebranded its services as part of a high profile marketing campaign, developed more frequent and reliable bus journeys, and introduced a flat fare of £1 for every bus journey,

with discounts for younger and older people. This has been supported by the council through the introduction of bus priority lanes and improvements to bus shelters, such as the provision of real-time information about bus waiting times. The council has also been seeking ways in which 'park and ride' measures can play a role in encouraging people to use bus services around the Brighton city area. Since the partnership began, the council has spent £35,000 per year on publicity and the bus company has spent £225,000 per year on its marketing and advertisements. The £2 million cost of the real time information systems has been shared between them. The locality has started to see the benefit in increased passenger numbers, with an average of a five per cent per year increase in bus patronage compared to 1994 levels – which is higher than the national average.

Source: Brighton and Hove City Council (2000 and 2003); DfT (2004g)

Car clubs

Car clubs give people access to a car without having to own it. Typically, car club members pay an annual membership fee to an operator and members then pay by the hour and mile when they use a vehicle. The combined costs of membership and use are intended to be cheaper than personal car ownership, for car owners who do not do a high mileage. As economies of scale are reached car clubs become self-financing so that, over the longer term, they require no public subsidy. The evidence suggests that car clubs are most effective in urban or residential areas where there is a restriction on car parking spaces or parking charges (DfT, 2004g). Car clubs should be promoted in conjunction with new developments in the South East, especially if there are a limited number of residential car parking places.

Transport and planning – designing sustainable communities

There are surprisingly few empirical studies about the relationship between land use patterns and traffic growth in Britain. A recent study argued that the significant growth in road traffic over recent decades far outweighs anything that could be attributed to changing patterns of land use (Headicar, 2003). Some planning policies have clearly encouraged the growth in traffic, such as the relaxation of planning controls during the 1980s that led to the proliferation of out-of-town commercial and retail developments. But development is an evolutionary process and many settlements have maintained their traditional compact character. This is not to negate the importance of development planning but to recognise its limitations.

Planning policies have the greatest potential in relation to major redevelopments or new developments, such as the growth areas in the South East. While compact and higher density developments help to sustain good coverage of local public transport services (Power, 2004), proximity to major regional centres also influences car dependency. The commuting patterns of two similar sized settlements in Oxfordshire illustrate the importance of proximity – Abingdon, seven miles from Oxford and Banbury, more than twenty miles from Oxford. In 2000, even though a higher proportion of people who lived in Banbury worked in their home town than was the case for Abingdon residents, the average commuting distance by car was much longer from Banbury (Headicar, 2000). This suggests that focusing new developments close to existing regional centres helps to reduce commuting distances, which is a proposal in the *South East Plan: Consultation Draft* (SEERA, 2005).

Traffic management and street design

Pedestrian casualties provide a hard measure of the impact of road traffic on quality of life. Research by ippr showed that children from the ten per cent most deprived wards in England were more than three times as likely to be pedestrian casualties as their counterparts from the least deprived ten per cent of wards, using the government's Index of Multiple Deprivation (IMD). This was compounded by the fact that more children live in deprived areas, so that there were eight times as many child pedestrian casualties in the most deprived tenth of wards, compared to the least deprived tenth (Grayling et al., 2002). This inequality also exists for adult pedestrians but is less pronounced.

Improving road safety education is clearly helpful and the Government has targeted extra resources at deprived areas for this purpose (DfT, 2004c). But changing the behaviour of drivers is likely to be more effective, in particular reducing the speeds in residential areas. For example, 20 mph zones combine the lower speed limit with humps or speed cushions and other changes to the road layout that make them self-enforcing. But road humps are an imperfect solution, creating their own problems of noise for residents and inconvenience for drivers. While cost effective and popular in many areas, they are not appropriate in all circumstances and unpopular in some local authorities. They might be seen as an evolutionary step, towards a new approach to traffic management in residential areas.

The traditional approach is that people and vehicles should be segregated, epitomised by the Buchanan report on traffic in towns that set the agenda for generations of traffic engineers (HMSO, 1963). A different approach, however, is to redesign streets in favour of pedestrians and cyclists, towards the reintegration of traffic and people on more equal terms. The development of 'home zones' represents the beginning of this movement in Britain. At lower speeds, 20 mph or preferably less, it seems possible to deregulate safely the traffic environment – for example, removing barriers, road markings and traffic lights – and for pedestrians, cyclists and motorists to negotiate shared use of road space through eye contact (Hamilton-Baillie, 2001). This approach is already well advanced in the Netherlands and Denmark, both of which have lower child pedestrian casualty rates than Britain.

Transport improvements and economic performance

The transport elements of the *South East Plan: Consultation Draft* are built around the idea of transport 'hubs' and 'spokes' as shown in Figure 9. Hubs are defined as settlements where the provision of (or potential to provide) a range of multi-modal transport services supports the concentration of 'high order' economic activity. Spokes are defined as transport corridors linking the hubs to enhance accessibility (SEERA, 2005).

The hubs are largely major urban commuter centres, such as Oxford and Guildford, and/or areas that have been identified as growth areas such as Milton Keynes and Ashford. The hubs could all be classified as areas of strong economic potential. As key locations for the movement of people and goods within the region it appears to make economic sense to focus some transport investment on further developing these areas.

The challenge facing the South East is how, and if, transport and hubs and spokes can be used for improving the economic performance of less prosperous areas in the South East. This could occur in two ways. First, by directing transport infrastructure investment to boost economic activity in disadvantaged areas, for example through building a new road. Second, by improving the transport services to and from areas where employment rates are low to facilitate labour mobility, for example by improving the reliability of existing local bus and train services.

The former was considered in a report by the Standing Advisory Committee on Trunk Road Assessment (SACTRA), commissioned by the Government, which examined the inter-relationship between transport improvements and economic activity. It concluded that, at the national level, there was limited potential in a developed economy like the UK's for transport improvements to deliver sustained benefits. For local schemes, it highlighted the need for a careful appraisal of the costs and benefits. That is, even where there is potential for transport improvements to improve economic efficiency overall, there may be winners and losers (DETR, 1999).

Figure 9: Regional hubs and spokes proposed by SEERA

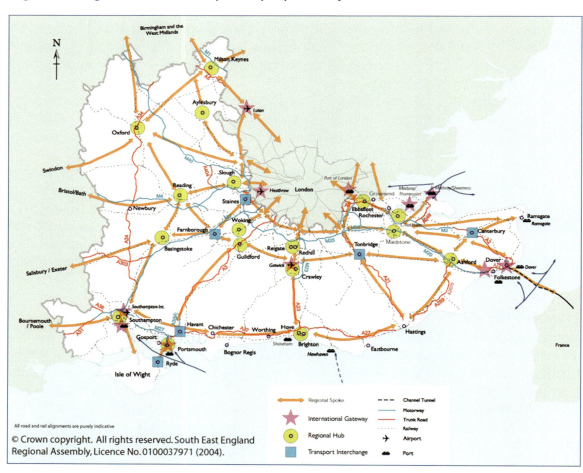

Source: SEERA, 2005

> **Hastings – options for transport improvements**
>
> Hastings is one of the least prosperous towns in the South East and has failed to attract inward investment or retain existing businesses. The contribution that various transport infrastructure improvements could make to Hastings has been considered in two Multi-Modal Studies. One of the options proposed was to construct a link road from Hastings to Bexhill, bypassing the seafront, although this was rejected by the Government on economic grounds since it would only serve to connect areas with similar levels of unemployment. A further option was to improve rail links into London and develop Hastings into a commuter town. Part of the premise behind the Sustainable Communities Plan was to create new growth areas in the South East and East of England to ease pressure on London for more resources, transport and housing. Investing in rail improvements that could potentially increase the numbers of people commuting from Hastings into London might work against this strategy. The Multi-Modal Studies recognised that attracting commuters to Hastings is likely to create increased demand for larger, family dwellings. But, as recognised in chapter 3, these may not be the kinds of homes that should be the priority for public subsidy in the South East, as they would not necessarily meet the affordable housing needs of the people already living in Hastings. In addition, improving rail links between London and Hastings would not necessarily help to create new employment opportunities for the residents of Hastings.
>
> Sources: Multi-Modal Study for Hastings (GOSE, 2000) and the South Coast Corridor Multi-Modal Study (GOSE, 2002)

The Hastings case study highlights that it is uncertain whether investing in transport infrastructure improvements will be beneficial to people living in less prosperous areas. The case for improving the reliability and quality of transport services between transport hubs and areas where employment rates are low appears to be stronger.

The East Kent and Ashford Sub-Regional Strategy (SEERA, 2005) highlighted that restricted accessibility of residents in the coastal towns to available employment opportunities has been exacerbated by poor quality public transport links. Intra-regional rail links are of particularly poor quality. The Strategy emphasised the importance of improving the transport services between deprived areas, such as Thanet, and major business and service centres, such as Ashford. Ashford has been identified as one of the transport hubs in the *South East Plan: Consultation Draft* and is one of the fastest growing towns in the South East. Making it easier for people in the coastal towns to reach employment opportunities in Ashford would not necessarily require major investments in transport infrastructure, but rather improvements to the quality of existing local rail and bus services.

Chapter 2 argued that the best way to reduce intra-regional disparities within the South East is to focus policy attention and resources on improving the employment rates within the region. Improving transport accessibility for people living in the South East's coastal towns could play an important role in opening up new employment opportunities to the people living in these less prosperous areas. The priority should be given to improving the reliability and quality of rail services within the South East.

Better co-ordinating transport policy and delivery

There is a need for better co-ordination of transport planning and delivery both within the South East and across the Greater South East.

A single 'Housing, Planning and Transport Regional Board'

One of the recommendations from Kate Barker's 'Review of Housing Supply' (Barker, 2004) was to integrate housing and planning decisions better at the regional level. The Government has accepted Barker's proposal to merge the current Regional Housing Boards and Regional Planning Bodies (ODPM, 2004). The appendix includes a summary of the current structure of the South East Committees and Regional Boards. The South East has been trialling an 'Experimental Regional Transport Board.' The Board has been chaired by an official from the Government Office for the South East (GOSE) which has raised some doubt about the extent to which the Government is genuinely interested in devolving transport decision making down to the regional and local levels.

A recent Government consultation considered how the regions could play a greater role in advising ministers on regional funding allocations for transport, housing and economic development. It proposed that regions should advise ministers, not only on strategic spending priorities within these three funding areas, but also on the distribution of funding between transport, housing and economic development. It suggested that 'in some cases a region may want to re-profile spending – by proposing changes to the funding in the three policy areas that off-set each other over a period of years – for example if there were a large transport scheme in an early period, and then a large housing scheme in a later period' (HMT/DfT/ODPM,DTI, 2004).

Bearing this in mind, there is merit for combining housing, planning and transport policy advice at the regional level through the creation of a single 'Housing, Planning and Transport Regional Board.' This single board could serve as the main body for advising ministers on strategic spending priorities across policy areas as well as the possibility of switching funding between them. Housing, Planning and Transport Regional Boards could offer several advantages:

A joining up of policy-making at the regional level
Rather than creating new Regional Transport Boards, it would make sense to join up the responsibilities for housing, planning and transport into a single board. The Sustainable Communities Plan (ODPM, 2003) has been criticised for not paying enough attention to whether additional transport infrastructure and services will be able to keep pace with the rate of new development. Creating a single regional board for housing, planning and transport would help to integrate strategic policy-making across these three areas.

Democratic accountability
The Housing, Planning and Transport Regional Board should be a multi-stakeholder body to avoid giving too much power to unelected officials and to ensure the legitimacy of any decisions that are made. As with the South East Planning Committee, the board's composition should reflect the balance on the Assembly of elected local authority representatives, alongside senior representatives from business, the environmental and voluntary sectors, and relevant agencies. The chair of the board should be a democratically elected representative. The Housing, Planning and

Transport Regional Board should be supported and advised by expert officials from the different agencies and authorities within the regions.

Streamlining governance arrangements

Housing, Planning and Transport Regional Boards could help to streamline and join up policy-making, not only within regions, but also between them. The structure of housing, planning and transport policy-making across the Greater South East is very complex. London, the South East and East of England regions currently all have separate boards and strategies for planning and housing. If the idea of Regional Transport Boards is taken forward, this would mean the creation of another regional board within each of the regions. Creating single Housing, Planning and Transport Regional Boards would make it much easier to better co-ordinate development and planning across the Greater South East.

Promoting subsidiarity

It is important to achieve a balance between local and regional tiers of decision making. Regional board structures should not suck up powers from the local level. The creation of Housing, Planning and Transport Regional Boards should not therefore lead to the erosion of existing local authority powers. Local authorities currently have responsibility for developing Local Transport Plans (LTPs) which reflect local transport priorities. Housing, Planning and Transport Regional Boards should account for the findings emerging from LTPs when advising ministers on spending priorities on behalf of the regions. In addition to providing spending advice, the Housing, Planning and Transport Regional Boards could also provide a vehicle for devolving some spending budgets. This could include the Community Infrastructure Fund (CIF), which is supporting transport infrastructure projects in the growth areas, and the Transport Innovation Fund (TIF), which is supporting traffic management projects in local areas.

A Greater South East Rail Authority

The South East Regional Transport Strategy highlights that radial movements into London are one of the major transport issues affecting the South East (GOSE, 2004). Table 4 shows the strong rail linkages between the South East, London and the East of England. It shows that virtually half of all rail journeys made in the South East have a destination within the Greater London boundary. The proportion is even higher for the East of England with two thirds of all rail journeys being London bound.

Table 4: Percentage of passenger journeys by rail from the East of England, London and South East in 2003-04

Origin	Destination								
	North East	North West	Yorkshire & the Humber	East Midlands	West Midlands	East of England	London	South East	South West
East of England	0%	0%	1%	1%	0%	29%	66%	2%	0%
London	0%	1%	1%	1%	1%	13%	65%	17%	1%
South East	0%	0%	0%	0%	1%	1%	49%	46%	2%

Source: SRA, 2003-04 cited in DfT, 2004b, Regional Transport Statistics

The concentration of rail passenger journeys within the administrative boundaries of London, the South East and East of England suggests that a new approach to strategic rail decision-making is needed for the Greater South East. Planning academics, such as Professor Peter Hall, have argued that commuter patterns across the Greater South East call for new governance arrangements for better planning transport provision, particularly in the case of rail services (Hall, 2004).

The 2004 Future of Rail White Paper announced many changes to the structure and organisation of the UK's railways, including the abolition of the Strategic Rail Authority. It also announced that greater powers are to be given to regional organisations (DfT, 2004h). The White Paper recognised that central government is not always best placed to take decisions on the transport needs of different communities and that, in future, the devolved administrations would take increased responsibilities for passenger services and, where appropriate, infrastructure. It proposed that the Scottish Executive and Welsh Assembly Government should be given franchising powers to set minimum service standards for train operators, including the frequency of train services and train operating contracts.

Transport for London (TfL) – an executive body directly accountable to the Mayor of London and not the GLA Assembly – has argued that, in addition to the other transport modes it already has responsibility for within London, it should also have control over rail services. It has proposed the creation of a London Regional Rail Authority which would cover suburban train services that extend beyond the Greater London boundary (TfL, 2005).

The 2005 Railways Act effectively paves the way for the creation of a London Regional Rail Authority. The Act states that TfL can enter into a franchise agreement if it is approved by the Secretary of State (House of Lords, 2005 – Clause 16). While the majority of London's workforce lives within Greater London, virtually all of London's remaining workforce are commuters from the South East and East of England (ONS, 2004b). The Act requires that the Mayor must ensure that 'at least two members of TfL are able to represent the interests of the persons living, working and studying in areas outside Greater London that are served by railway passenger services in respect of which TfL carries out functions…' It also requires the 'the Mayor must consult with the regional planning body for each of the regions' when selecting the two extra board members (House of Lords, 2005 – Clause 17).

This model has some advantages. It means that local and regional rail services can be integrated with the road and public transport services which TfL already has responsibility for in Greater London, including the London Underground, light rail and bus services. It also gives responsibility for planning rail services to an executive body in TfL that has the professional capacity to take them on. However, even with an extra two members, the TfL board will still be dominated by people representing London's interests and not the South East's or East of England's. Moreover, with the exception of the Mayor of London, the board of TfL is not elected.

An alternative proposal would be to devolve responsibility for the franchising of rail passenger services to a new Greater South East Rail Authority. It would make sense that TfL is still the executive body responsible for implementing the decisions of the authority, in the same way that Passenger Transport Executives implement the decisions of Passenger Transport Authorities in the metropolitan areas. This would keep the opportunity to integrate services, including fares, timetables, ticketing and passenger information. TfL's broader remit might eventually justify a change in its name. The new rail authority would have responsibility for ensuring a high quality and co-ordinated rail service is provided for passengers across the Greater South East. But it would not have a remit over inter-city rail journeys, which would remain the responsibility of the Department for Transport (DfT).

To ensure democratic accountability, the new rail authority should be governed by a board of politically elected representatives who would be supported and advised by officials – in the same way that Passenger Transport Authorities consist of councillors from the constituent metropolitan district councils. Local politicians from all three regions – London, the South East and East of England – could be nominated onto the board. In London, the nominations could be made by the Mayor from the Greater London Assembly. The new rail authority would need to work closely with both TfL and Network Rail, which is responsible for operating and maintaining the rail network.

Key findings

The transport challenge

- There has been a legacy of under-spending on transport in the UK.

- Public spending on transport will be limited over the coming years. The South East, like every region, will find it increasingly difficult to find the resources necessary to fund transport improvements.

- Road traffic could rise by 25 per cent in the South East by 2010 (from 2000).

Road user charging and funding transport improvements

- Significant upfront investment in transport infrastructure is needed to secure public support for a national congestion charging scheme.

- A national congestion charging scheme, introduced on a revenue raising basis (on top of existing motoring taxes), could help to reduce the rate of traffic growth in the South East by nine per cent by 2010.

- Congestion charging could free up extra revenue for much needed transport improvements, but it could take ten years before a national scheme is technically feasible.

- If politicians are to win public support for national congestion charging, in the preceding years there will need to be increased public spending on transport to offer accessible, reliable and cost-effective transport options.

- Increased transport investment could be financed through higher public borrowing. The future burden of interest payments could be partly met from the revenue raised from a national congestion charging scheme.

- Some of the future revenue raised from motorists should be redistributed back to the regions. But there is a trade-off between using the revenue gains from a national congestion charging scheme to fund upfront transport investment initially financed through borrowing, and using the revenue to pay for transport improvements in future decades. There needs to be a balance between the two.

Short to medium term pathways for cutting congestion

- Local urban charging schemes should be implemented in some of the South East's busiest centres. Local authorities will need funding for packages of measures that combine road pricing with local public transport improvements.

- There should be motorway tolling on congested commuter routes, as well as tolling on major motorway sections that are due to be widened. Motorway tolling schemes could be introduced as public-private partnerships.

- Local urban charging and motoring tolling schemes should exempt cleaner vehicles that produce less greenhouse gas emissions.

Transport and planning – smarter measures and sustainable community design

- Smarter travel measures, such as travel plans and public transport marketing, could have a considerable impact on reducing the rate at which traffic is set to increase and should be scaled up without delay.

- A new approach to traffic management should be encouraged where residential streets are redesigned in favour of pedestrians and cyclists.

- Improving transport accessibility for people living in the South East's coastal towns could play an important role in opening up new employment opportunities to the people living in these less prosperous areas. The priority should be given to improving intra-regional rail links.

Co-ordinating transport policy and delivery

- A single 'Housing, Planning and Transport Regional Board' should be created for advising ministers on spending priorities across policy areas, as well as the possibility of switching funding between them.

- A Greater South East Rail Authority should be created with responsibility for the franchising of rail passenger services across the Greater South East (excluding intercity rail journeys).

5. Troubled waters? Water resources and flooding in the South East

The effects of water shortages and flooding in the South East will almost certainly intensify over future decades with climate change, increased development and changing lifestyles. The South East is one of the driest regions in Britain but has high rates of per capita consumption (pcc) of water compared to other English regions (Environment Agency, 2004a). While there is potentially enough water to meet rising demand for new housing and domestic consumption, this will only be possible with the timely provision of new water resources and significantly higher water efficiency savings in existing and new homes. As identified in chapter 4, if the South East is to manage demand for road transport, it will need to influence the behaviour of individuals and firms through road user charging and smarter travel options. Similarly, encouraging more efficient water use will require higher levels of metering in areas of low water availability; minimum standards for household water efficiency; and better co-ordination of water resource management and development planning.

By 2080, the number of people at risk from flooding in the South East is expected to be higher than today (Foresight, 2004). Despite planning policy guidance directing development away from areas at risk of flooding, inappropriate development is still occurring. In the South East growth areas, 30 per cent of the development sites planned for 2016-31 will be in flood risk areas. However, the majority will be in areas where the probability of flooding is either low or moderate (ABI, 2005). Across all the growth areas, flood management measures will need to be periodically reviewed to ensure a high standard of protection.

This chapter sets out to address two key questions:

■ Is there enough water to meet the rising demand for new housing and domestic consumption in the South East?

■ What impact will new housing developments have on flood risk in the South East growth areas?

This chapter focuses on household use of water. (Refer to Environment Agency (2001) for information on other demands for water from the agricultural, commercial and industrial sectors in the South East.) Water quality is not a strong focus, although it is considered alongside water resources. In terms of assessing flood risk, we have focused on the growth areas. While water resources and flooding are treated separately, we recognise their inter-relatedness. Measures to tackle flooding can contribute to improvements in water supply and quality, while some water efficiency measures can reduce the impact of development on flood risk.

Pressures on the water environment

Some of the factors affecting the water environment include population growth, development, public attitudes, changing lifestyles and climate change. As examined in chapter 3, the South East has been experiencing fairly strong population and housing growth. The development of the South East growth areas will in turn impact on the availability of water resources, water quality and flood risk. But much can be done to reduce the negative impacts through careful siting and design of new development.

Chapter 1 identified that people's awareness of future environmental risks in the South East, such as water shortages and flooding, is limited. But recent research suggests that housebuyers are willing to spend more on sustainable homes, including measures to reduce water use (Mulholland Research and Consulting, 2004). Research on attitudes to flooding indicates that people have unrealistic expectations of the role and capacity of the Government and other public agencies to deal with hazards. A widely held view among members of the public, is that floods can be eradicated or that defences should be erected on all floodplains, regardless of the costs and benefits (Brown and Damery, 2002). The Government and other public agencies will need to raise awareness of the longer-term risks of flooding, so that people can make informed choices about the extent they are willing to accept these future risks.

Over the coming decades, climate change will present many potential challenges to the water environment in the South East. During the 20th Century the South East's average surface temperature rose by 0.5 degrees Celsius (°C). The UK Climate Impacts Programme projects that we are committed to further climate change for the next 30-40 years as a result of past greenhouse gas emissions and inertia in the climate system (UKCIP, 2002). The South East could face warmer, wetter and more variable winters and hotter, drier summers with up to a 60 per cent decrease in precipitation and temperatures up to 5°C warmer (UKCIP, 2002). Sea level in the South East could rise between 26cm and 86cm above current levels, and coastal erosion is likely to substantially increase (Foresight, 2004). Changing rainfall patterns and rising sea level will increase the risk of flooding along rivers, coasts and in urban areas where high intensity rains can quickly overwhelm inadequate drainage systems. Drier summers will have implications for the supply of water, the maintenance of river flows and the ability of receiving waters to receive effluent. Although the impacts of climate change are uncertain, a precautionary approach is advisable.

The South East water balance

The South East is a water stressed region. During a dry year, current levels of water abstraction are having damaging impacts on rivers, and in several areas there is now a presumption against issuing new licences for summer water abstractions. The most significant abstractor of water, at 47 per cent, is the Public Water Supply (PWS), which is water supplied by water companies to customers. The region is heavily dependent on groundwater, with 60 per cent of PWS abstraction in the Environment Agency's Southern Region taken from chalk aquifers, compared to ten per cent from reservoirs and ten per cent from direct river abstraction (Environment Agency, 2001).

PWS stress occurs when there are problems meeting the supply-demand balance and this can relate to average or peak demand[6], which usually occurs in the summer when demand is high and supplies are low. On the Office of Water Service's (Ofwat) security of supply index, only two South East water companies (Portsmouth and Sutton and East Surrey) currently achieve the top 'A' rating, indicating no deficit against target headroom[7]. But three companies: Southern, Folkestone and Dover, and Thames have the lowest 'D' rating, indicating large deficits against target headroom (Ofwat, 2004a). While customers should not expect immediate supply problems, the company is operating with a greater than planned likelihood on needing to apply restrictions during a dry year.

Figure 1: Current water resources surplus – deficit forecast (2005)

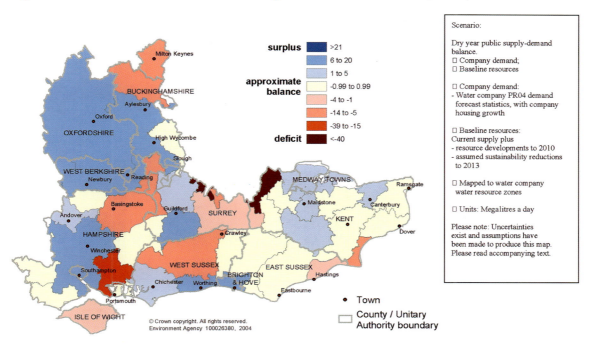

Source: WRSE Group, 2004

The water companies have drought plans agreed with the Environment Agency, but following the 1995 drought, water companies are hesitant to apply customer water use restrictions (Thames Water Utilities, 2004), and the Government has not encouraged the use of Drought Orders or Drought Permits that impact the environment (DETR and Welsh Office, 1999). Figure 1 shows the 2005 water resources supply-deficit forecast. It indicates which areas are more likely to be in deficit if the year is dry. Indications are that 2005 will be dry owing to low winter rainfall. Many water companies in the South East, including those with 'A' security of supply ratings, have started to enact drought plans (Environment Agency, 2005a).

6   In the Environment Agency Southern Region four out of five water companies regard planning and investing for peak period to be at least as necessary as for the annual average supply-demand. Peaks are estimated to be an important determinant in up to 90 per cent of a water undertaker's new capital expenditures and responsible for much of the forecast growth of public water supply in England and Wales (Herrington, 1998).

7   In water company planning, supply is planned to meet forecast demand plus 'headroom'. Headroom is used to allow for uncertainties in supply and demand levels and 'target headroom' is the minimum amount of headroom that a company should incorporate into its plans. This has typically been in the range of five to ten per cent of available supplies over demand (Environment Agency, 2001), but varies between resource zones reflecting different levels of uncertainty.

Accounting for water use

Households account for the majority of PWS demand – 57 per cent in England and Wales, while total leakage accounts for 23 per cent of water distributed (Ofwat, 2004a). The pcc for both unmetered and metered households has increased steadily over time. However, different water companies report different figures for pcc, and some of the higher pcc figures may be disguising higher rates of leakage, which are being underestimated by the companies (ENDS Report, 2004). Average pcc for the South East (for both metered and unmetered households) is significantly higher than the average for England and Wales (Figure 2) (Ofwat, 2004a). Leaving aside under-reporting of leakage, just why water consumption continues to grow or why it so high in the South East is poorly understood. One of the most significant factors thought to determine water consumption in the UK is household size (Thames Water Utilities, 2004), with socio-economic factors such as income and type of area also found to be significant (Edwards and Martin, 1995).

Figure 2: Per capita consumption (pcc) of water for households: average for the South East and England and Wales, 2004

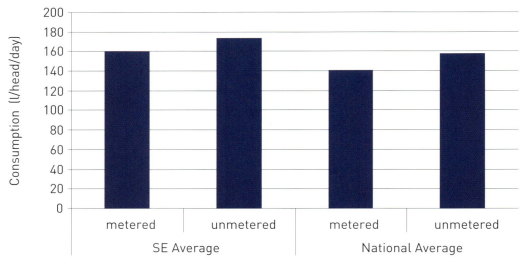

Source: Ofwat, 2004a

Note: The South East figures are an aggregate of: Southern, Thames, Folkestone and Dover, Mid-Kent, Portsmouth, South East, Sutton and East Surrey, and Three Valleys. Metered households tend to consume less water per head due to a combination of two factors – 1. metered households tend to be more efficient; 2. more efficient households tend to opt for metering.

Total industry leakage rates increased over the last three years following a period of reduction from a peak in 1995 (Ofwat, 2004a). Figure 3 shows that Thames Water has the worst absolute leakage record. In 2003-04, its leakage levels stabilised after a rise in 2002-03, but were still higher than any other company whether measured on an absolute or per property basis (Ofwat, 2004a). Ofwat sets mandatory target levels for leakage, based on the Economic Level of Leakage (ELL).[8] In the South East, Thames Water and Three Valleys Water have failed to reach their leakage targets, with Thames Water having the biggest leakage reductions to make during 2005-10 (20 per cent on current levels).

---

8   This is the level at which it would cost more to make further reductions than to produce the water from another source, and operating at the ELL helps ensure best value for customers.

Figure 3: Company estimates of total leakage (l/prop/day), 2004

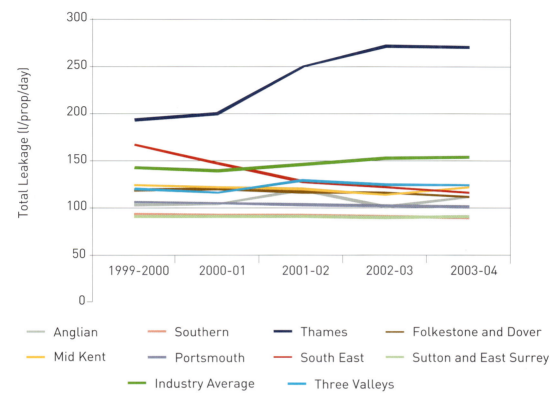

Legend:
- Anglian
- Mid Kent
- Industry Average
- Southern
- Portsmouth
- Three Valleys
- Thames
- South East
- Folkestone and Dover
- Sutton and East Surrey

Source: Ofwat, 2004a

Water quality

After significant improvements over the last decade, there has been a recent decline in the chemical and biological quality of South East rivers. Increased development, combined with unregulated diffuse pollution sources, threatens continued improvements to water quality, with a major obstacle to greater regulatory control being the difficulty in quantifying the contribution of diffuse pollution to the deterioration of river quality.

The presumption in Planning and Development Control has been that pollution problems can be solved by the installation of appropriate treatment facilities or technologies, and therefore should not impede development. However, with the expected increases in development in the South East, and higher building standards having little to no effect on water quality problems, future protection of the water environment cannot be secured on this basis. Proactive planning will be essential to secure the necessary water infrastructure.

Some sewage treatment works (STW) in the South East have reached, or are nearing, the point where currently available technology is not adequate to secure the effluent quality needed to maintain environmental water quality. Other STWs have limited capacity to deal with additional housing growth (above RPG9) without the need for high additional investment. The location and phasing of new housing development will be critical. Some locations may not be able to respond to increased growth levels in the short term due to the lead times needed to deliver the necessary infrastructure, and a few sites may not be able to accept any new development due to the fragility of the water environment. The Environment Agency is working with SEERA, Southern Water and Thames Water to identify sensitive sites and work out the appropriate location, phasing and funding of infrastructure needed to accommodate housing growth. This work must be done in time to feed into the South East Plan.

Water Resources in the South East (WRSE) group report

The Water Resources in the South East (WRSE) Group is a technical group consisting of representatives from water companies, the Department for Environment, Food and Rural Affairs (Defra), SEERA, Ofwat, Watervoice, English Nature and chaired by the Environment Agency. To guide the preparation of the *South East Plan: Consultation Draft*, the Group produced a report exploring the impact of various housing growth scenarios on the PWS balance (WRSE Group, 2004). The report's key message was that 'increased demand from new development in the South East can only be accommodated through a combination of demand and supply side activities'. However, the report did not consider the housing growth impacts from surrounding regions, including London. It is unclear how much of London's water demand is met from water resources in the South East and if this will increase in the future.

The report was based on a number of assumptions, some of which are optimistic. If they do not materialise, very different outcomes could be reached:

■ Appropriate planning permissions and abstraction licences for supply side options are delivered in a timely way. But abstraction licenses need to be approved by the Environment Agency and reservoirs can take years to plan and are often opposed by local communities.

■ Enabling mechanisms to encourage greater demand management (e.g. water efficiency fittings in new homes). But take-up of water efficiency measures will be low without regulations or financial incentives to encourage them.

■ Over 55 per cent of the households in the SEERA region will be metered by 2020. This is an optimistic assumption as most South East water companies are failing to meet their metering targets.

■ The impacts of climate change are no greater than allowed for in the modelling. But there are still uncertainties surrounding future predictions of the impact of climate change, particularly at the regional level.

■ Adequate funding will be provided to implement water resource plans. But long term funding for water infrastructure is not necessarily certain.

The report was updated in April 2005 (WRSE Group, 2005) to take account of different housing growth scenarios presented as options in the *South East Plan: Consultation Draft*. In the 2004 report, two housing growth rates and water efficiency projections were modelled. The annual housing growth scenarios were: 29,500 and 36,000. However, the 36,000 annual housing growth rate was rejected by the South East Assembly. The upper annual housing growth rate proposed by the *South East Plan: Consultation Draft* is 32,000 (SEERA, 2005). In the 2005 report the annual housing growth rates modelled were 25,500 and 32,000. In addition the 2005 report modelled the growth rates using the sub-regional distribution of housing growth, rather than the even distribution assumed in the 2004 report. This distribution proved more compatible with water company plans and the report states that it should therefore be less costly to provide a secure water supply than the 2004 report suggested.

The two water efficiency scenarios examined in both reports were: a conservative eight per cent reduction in pcc in new homes, assumed to be possible through expected changes to the Building Regulations; and 21 per cent reduction in pcc in new homes, considered achievable with the installation of the full range of water efficient devices and appliances. Water efficiency savings in existing homes and from other sectors were not considered. For all the scenarios examined, the modelling assumed that three quarters of the projected deficit is met from new supplies, such as reservoirs, while a quarter is met from demand management measures.

Figure 4 shows the 2025 water resources surplus-deficit forecast if there is an annual housing growth rate of 32,000 per year (using a sub-regional distribution of housing growth), new water resource provision and an eight per cent reduction in pcc in new homes. This scenario would put the region's water surplus-deficit largely in balance, with some surpluses in parts of the region. However, other scenarios paint a very different picture.

Figure 4: Projected water resources surplus-deficit forecast, 2025: 32,000 annual housing growth rate (sub-regional distribution of housing growth), further water resources and an eight per cent reduction in pcc in new homes.

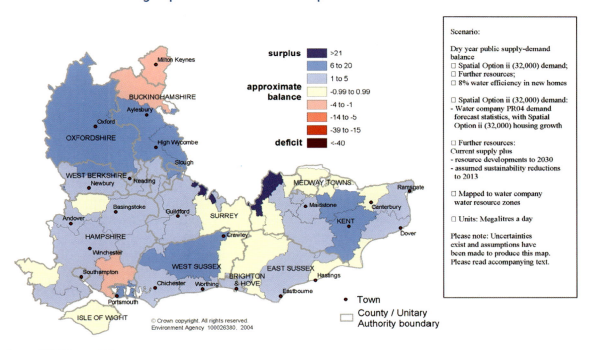

Source: WRSE Group, 2005

Figure 5 shows a 'worse case' scenario for 2025, with an annual housing growth rate of 29,500 dwellings a year, no new water resources and no improvement in water efficiency. The annual housing growth rate could be higher than this at 32,000 dwellings per year, but the distribution of the housing across the different sub-regions will be more favourable to a positive water surplus-deficit forecast than that indicated in Figure 5 (WRSE Group, 2005).

Figure 5: Projected water resources surplus-deficit forecast, 2025: 29,500 annual housing growth rate (spread evenly across the region), no new water resources and no improvement in water efficiency.

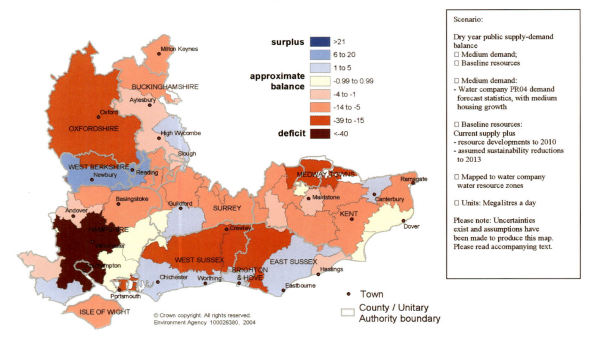

Source: WRSE Group, 2004

Nonetheless, Figure 5 shows that without new resources or improvements in water efficiency, significant parts of the region would be in deficit by 2025, with parts of Hampshire severely in deficit. This would result in a very fragile water balance, heavily susceptible to dry years, with hosepipe bans, standpipes and other drought measures becoming a more frequent occurrence, which would have impacts for the economy and public health and put the water environment at risk of serious long-term damage.

Figure 6 shows that an annual housing growth of 32,000 dwellings a year – if accompanied by further water resources and a 21 per cent reduction in pcc in new homes – would result in water surpluses across the region by 2025. As the WRSE Group 2005 report states, such surpluses may represent an unnecessary use of resources, and so some resource developments could be deferred. It must be remembered, however, that this modelling does not consider the impacts of housing growth from London and other regions, which may need the surpluses indicated above.

These scenarios indicate that whatever level of housing growth is decided upon, it will *only* be possible to accommodate significant new housing if there are both new resources and, at the very least, an eight per cent reduction in pcc in new homes. If higher rates of water efficiency are achieved in new and existing homes then some resource developments can be deferred. This will require enabling mechanisms to be in place to allow water efficiency savings to be realised (WRSE Group, 2005). The recent update by

Figure 6: Projected water resources surplus-deficit forecast, 2025: 32,000 annual housing growth rate (sub-regional distribution of housing growth), further water resources and a 21 per cent reduction in pcc in new homes.

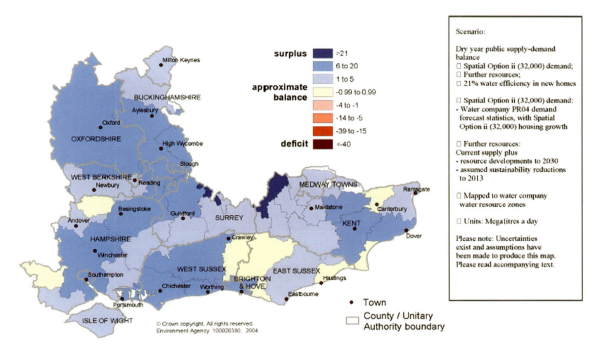

Source: WRSE Group, 2005

the WRSE Group (2005) demonstrated that the sub-regional location of new development should result in a more favourable water balance than was first feared. But it is still unclear what effects the sub-regional distribution of housing will have on water quality.

The WRSE Group's modelling assumes that new resources will be ready before demand outstrips supply. But proceeding with higher housebuilding rates, on the assumption that new resources will be delivered to meet rising demand, is a risky strategy. Reservoirs are not 'quick fixes' and can take 15 to 20 years to implement (HoC Environment, Food and Rural Affairs Select Committee, 2004). The gaining of planning permission cannot be assumed, as there is often significant local public opposition to new reservoir developments. A most recent example has been the vetoing of planning permission for a desalination plant at Beckton by the Mayor of London.

The assumptions underlying the WRSE Group's approach to assessing the future water supply-deficit need to be reviewed, to be more cautious about supply side solutions to meeting future water needs in the South East. To ensure that the rate of new housebuild does not outstrip water supply in the region, it would be advisable to aim for higher savings from water efficiency from both new and existing homes and avoid locating strategic developments in water stressed areas.

Achieving a sustainable water balance in the South East

The Government's Sustainable Development Strategy, which recognises the concept of environmental limits, commits to pursuing development in ways that will protect and enhance the physical and natural environment, and use resources and energy as efficiently as possible (Defra, 2005a). To this end, the Government advocates a twin-track approach to managing water supplies, where new resource developments are selected as an option, only where a demand management approach is clearly insufficient or unjustified in terms of cost. However, the Environment Agency criticised the plans produced by the water companies for the 2004 periodic review for being dominated by resource development rather than demand management (Environment Agency, 2004b).

As identified in chapter 1, it will become increasingly difficult for the region to offer its citizens a high quality of life, without offsetting policy measures for changing the behaviour of individuals and firms. One reason given for the imbalance between new supplies and demand management is that demand management is seen as more uncertain than supply augmentation. Changing individual behaviour to encourage greater water efficiency will rely on the co-operation of householders and it is difficult to predict the savings that could be achieved. Furthermore, it has been suggested that there are greater financial incentives for water companies to acquire more assets than there are to manage demand and that no funding is allocated for managing demand.

The next section considers a balanced way of managing water resources in the South East based on a combination of two approaches: increasing water supply and managing demand for water. To readdress the imbalance between supply and demand side measures, this section focuses on demand management options in new and existing homes through widespread metering.

Increasing supply

The WRSE Group report (2004) revealed that even a 21 per cent reduction in pcc in new homes would be insufficient to accommodate future water needs under the 29,500 annual housing growth scenario. Further water resources would also be required. This section will not explore particular options, but consider the costs of new water infrastructure and options for better co-ordinating water resource planning with development planning.

Costing new water infrastructure

The case for water is different from other infrastructure considerations, such as transport, as the costs of providing new water infrastructure will be borne by individual customers through their water bills and by developer contributions. The Government is not expected to identify the funding necessary to meet additional water infrastructure costs. However, there will be ramifications for water bills in the South East. Water companies can recover from the developer some of the costs of making new connections and upgrading the local networks, and this is reflected in the price limits set by Ofwat. Ofwat expects such contributions to be in the region of £800 million (for England and Wales) over the next five years (Ofwat, 2005a). If water resources are already fully committed, or if the capacity of sewage treatment plants needs to be increased, there will be additional costs, paid by the customer base.

Table 1 shows the additional water and sewerage costs associated with new housing developments in the South East accounted for in the 2005-10 Water Price Review period. Ofwat expects 291,000 new connections for the water service will be needed in the region in this period, and this includes a consideration of the impact of the Sustainable Communities Plan (Ofwat, 2005b).

Table 1: The additional costs for water and sewerage services spread over the five-year period from 2005 to 2010

Water service	Total costs (£ million)	Cost per property (£)
South East	£288	£992
Rest of England and Wales	£397	£610
Sewerage service		
South East	£119	£429
Rest of England and Wales	£216	£345

Source: Ofwat, 2005b

Table 2 shows how these costs will be passed onto household water bills over the period 2005-2010. The bill increases range from £2 to £22 (spread over the five-year period) and will likely have a limited impact on customers, both in terms of affordability and in terms of encouraging water efficiency. Due to future housing numbers being undecided at the time of the Water Price Review, it remains unclear if that provided for in the Review is enough to maintain security of supply and water quality, particularly over the medium to long term.[9] Ofwat has recognised that, as water resources are stretched in the South East, one-off investments may be required in the medium term for large-scale assets such as reservoirs, which would increase water bills.

Table 2: Additional cost to household water bills in the South East spread over the five-year period from 2005 to 2010

	Water	Sewerage
Southern Water	£10	£2
Thames Water	£22	£7
Folkestone and Dover Water	£18	n/a
Mid Kent Water	£16	n/a
Portsmouth Water	£2	n/a
South East Water	£9	n/a
Sutton and East Surrey Water	£5	n/a
Three Valleys Water	£8	n/a

Source: Ofwat, 2005b

Co-ordinating water resource management and development planning

Because water resources could be irreparably damaged by over-exploitation, particularly in dry and densely populated regions such as the South East, better co-ordination between water resource management and development planning is essential. Currently PWS management is conducted on a rigid five-yearly cycle that does not match planning periods. Development plans should be developed in tandem with water resource plans, and both should consider long-term climate change impacts. For this to happen, water companies should be made statutory consultees for both Regional Spatial Strategies (RSSs) and Local Development Frameworks (LDFs), to ensure that the cost and limits of water infrastructure requirements are fully understood. Similarly, regulatory funding

---

9   It is known that the price determinations did allow studies to begin on two reservoirs in the South East and for further development of desalination plants at Beckton and Newhaven (Ofwat, 2004b).

cycles should be reconsidered. The benefits of this approach have been demonstrated by SEERA, who proactively work with water companies and the regulators through the WRSE Group. This has helped to co-ordinate the development of the *South East Plan: Consultation Draft* with water resource planning.

A further step towards a more integrated land-use and water planning system would be planning guidance on development and water issues. This could be a new Planning Policy Statement (PPS) on water resources, or alternatives could include broadening PPS 23 on planning and pollution control, or a PPS on environmental hazards to include flooding and other hazards such as contaminated land (Rydin, 2004). Both the availability of water resources and the impact on water quality over the lifetime of the development should be material considerations in development planning. Water scarcity and water quality should be grounds for refusal of planning permission in cases where further resources or improvements in water efficiency cannot be identified.

Managing demand for water

Reducing leakage

One way to improve the efficiency of existing water use is to reduce the amount of leakage. If water companies consistently fail to meet their water targets then Ofwat has enforcement powers under the Water Industry Act 1991. Ofwat has stated that it would use these 'as a last resort, to be triggered when there is a clear breach, and when it will produce results for customers more reliably and more quickly than less formal procedures' (Ofwat, 2005a). The high level of leakage in the Thames Water area has strengthened calls for Ofwat to enforce leakage targets more rigorously in order to reduce wastage. Clear penalties for failure would not only improve leakage rates, but provide a strong message to all water users on the seriousness of the water situation and the need to reduce wastage.

Leakage targets are set on the basis of the Economic Level of Leakage (ELL). As part of the recent price review, Ofwat asked all water companies to update their ELL appraisals. There is an on-going debate about how environmental and social considerations should be measured and incorporated within ELL.

Extending water metering

Approximately 76 per cent of domestic customers in England and Wales do not have a meter (Ofwat, 2004a) and pay for water on a fixed rate, where the bill is divided into a standing charge and an additional charge based on the rateable value of the home.[10] This contrasts with other utilities, such as gas and electricity, which are paid for on a unit basis, which encourages people to use the utility more efficiently. A survey for SEERA found that 84 per cent of residents said they would be willing to use less water (MORI, 2004). Water company research has estimated that voluntary water metering could reduce consumption by between two and 14 per cent per annum, with an average of nine per cent per annum (Environment Agency, 2004a). Logic suggests this would be higher for compulsory metering and if tariffs were designed to penalise excessive use. Metering is particularly effective at reducing peak demand for water.

---

10 These charges vary throughout England and Wales as some water companies make the standing charge the main element of the bill, while other makes the rateable value the main element. Rateable values were last assessed in 1991 and so they currently bear little relation to present property values.

Ofwat has estimated that the cost of an optional meter is about £194, and £237 for compulsory metering and metering on change of occupancy, with costs slightly higher in the South East (Ofwat, 2005b). There are cheaper ways of saving water through the use of some water conservation measures like variable flush devices, installed on a replacement basis. But it is not clear why people would be persuaded to install such devices if they have no incentive to do so. Water metering would enable people to save money by using less water and encourage people to use water efficient appliances in their homes.

The Water Industry Act 1999 forbids compulsory metering except in designated water scarce areas, and for customers with high water-using facilities such as power showers (HoC, 1998). Water companies now put meters into all new homes as a matter of course and can install them in properties at change of occupancy. The Act introduced the right to free domestic meter installation, which has encouraged more households to install meters. These measures have seen water companies in the South East increase metering rates since 1997/1998 (Environment Agency, 2004b) with 24 per cent of households in England and Wales metered in 2003/4 (Ofwat, 2004a). Nonetheless, as Table 3 shows, there are wide variations in the current and projected metering rates between water companies. For example Anglian Water achieved a near 50 per cent metering rate in 2003, demonstrating that significant penetration is already possible, while Portsmouth and Sutton and East Surrey are only forecast to achieve metering rates of 39 per cent and 44 per cent respectively by 2030.

Table 3: Water company household metering penetration 2003, 2010 and 2030

| Water Company | Meter penetration (%) | | |
	2003 (actual)	2010 (target)	2030 (target)
Anglian	49	64	90
Bournemouth and West Hampshire	**27**	**54**	**86**
Bristol	18	29	46
Cambridge	49	61	84
Choderton and District	13	22	No forecast supplied
Dee Valley	27	43	69
Welsh	14	31	61
Essex and Suffolk	30	46	69
Folkestone & Dover	**34**	**65**	**91**
Mid Kent	**27**	**44**	**74**
Northumbrian	8	20	43
Portsmouth	**3**	**12**	**39**
Severn Trent	21	31	66
South East	**25**	**37**	**63**
South Staffordshire	12	21	35
South West	36	64	90
Southern	**23**	**42**	**71**
Sutton and East Surrey	**16**	**25**	**44**
Tendring Hundred	54	66	85
Thames	**19**	**27**	**59**
Three Valleys	**18**	**43**	**81**
United Utilities	12	26	56
Wessex	28	44	73
Yorkshire	22	34	60

Source: Environment Agency (2004b) Meter penetration numbers can vary depending on whether household voids have been included in the calculation. The main water companies supplying the South East have been bolded.

The WRSE Group report assumes that over 55 per cent of households in the South East region will be metered by 2020 (WRSE Group, 2004), but most water companies supplying the South East are not on track to meet their targets. Unless companies take a more positive attitude to increasing metering in the region, it is unlikely that they will reach their forecasted metering rates (Environment Agency, 2004a). Ofwat must play a more prominent role in encouraging water companies to increase their metering rates.

One way forward would be for water companies to seek the designation of supply zones as 'Water Scarce Areas'. This would enable them to move more quickly towards higher metering rates where need is most urgent. To date, water companies have been reluctant to seek the designation, with Folkestone and Dover the only company currently considering it. The Environment Agency has advised that other parts of Kent, East Sussex and perhaps West Sussex may need to declare water scarcity status in the coming years (Environment Agency, 2001). As the regulatory body responsible for water abstractions and environmental protection, the Environment Agency should be given a stronger role in independently assessing when areas should be declared as Water Scarce, so that higher levels of metering can be advocated.

Water metering, fairness and affordability

The fixed rate method of charging householders for water in England and Wales is inefficient. As the bill is based on the rateable value rather than the volume used, two neighbouring homes can end up paying similar bills regardless of whether one household uses more or less water than the other.

However, there are concerns that the current system of optional metering is regressive – people who take it up are more likely to be small households in larger properties on generally higher incomes. To encourage a switch to metering, the administrative costs of metering and bills are not borne by those who are metered, but shared amongst all customers so that those who are unmetered effectively subsidise those who are. Since those who opt for voluntary metering tend to be better off and living in high rateable value homes, this tends to mean that poorer consumers subsidise richer consumers (NCC, 2002). But the current system, in which rateable value charges are used, is littered with questionable cross-subsidies. For instance, households in rural areas tend to pay less and so are subsidised by households in urban areas. Policies to encourage lower to middle income households to switch to metering would help to ensure that the administrative costs of metering are more equitably spread across different household income groups.

A recent study examined the distributional effects of various universal water metering and charging options (Ekins and Dresner, 2004). The analysis, which used data from Anglian Water, focused on whether, on average, households in the lower income bands (less than £10,000 and between £10,000 and £20,000) would be better or worse off with the introduction of metering. Due to a concern that metering could potentially result in poorer households sacrificing hygiene to save money (Fitch and Price, 2002), the study incorporated some metering options that combined an allowance of water at fixed cost to cover essential water uses. Some of the metering options explored differentiate between households on the basis of Council Tax bands, but because the way in which council tax is paid bears little relation to current property values, Council Tax bands were stretched so that the amount paid was roughly proportional to the value of the property in 1991. Three of the options are presented in Table 4.

Table 4: Metering options based on the Anglian Water tariff

Metering options	Household income < £10,000		Household incomes of £10,000-£20,000		Household incomes > £40,000	
	Average loss or gain (£ per week)	Proportion losing more than £1 per week (%)	Average loss or gain (£ per week)	Proportion losing more than £1 per week (%)	Average loss or gain (£ per week)	Proportion losing more than £1 per week (%)
Option 1: Metering with the existing Anglian Water tariff (no effect on existing metered customers).	+0.34	8	-0.02	15	-0.09	17
Option 2: Metering with the volumetric rate varying according to stretched Council Tax bands.	+1.09	6	+0.81	12	-0.36	37
Option 3: Metering with a fixed allowance of 20m³ per capita for the first adult and each child, and increased price per litre of water.	+0.31	12	+0.01	15	-0.17	25

Source: Ekins and Dresner, JRF (2004)

Table 4 shows that all the metering options investigated are progressive from the point of view of the lowest income households and all but one (option 1) are progressive for the next income group (£10,000 to £20,000). The table shows that all the options are unattractive from the point of view of the richest household income group (£40,000 and above). While option 2 leaves the fewest households in the two lowest income groups worst off, it leaves the highest proportion of households (37 per cent) worst off in the £40,000 and above income group.

As different water companies structure charges in different ways, Ekins and Dresner tested their metering options with Severn Trent, which is unique among water companies because customers pay no standing charge. This showed similar results indicating that the findings were not a function of the Anglian tariff. Although the study did not examine water companies in the South East, the results are likely to be representative. The study therefore supports the view that water metering would be progressive from the point of view of low income households in the South East.

Under the Water Industry (Charges) Vulnerable Groups Regulations that came into force in April 2000, vulnerable and low-income groups identified as having high essential water use can have their bills capped. A recent Select Committee on Water Pricing criticised the low take-up of the scheme – only 1.4 per cent take-up among eligible customers in 2001-2. It highlighted that the scheme had been less than effective because it does not reflect the large regional variations in water charges. The amount of means-tested benefit that householders receive is fixed, but water charges are not uniform. Consequently, the current assistance has largely been ineffective at tackling water affordability issues (HoC Environment, Food and Rural Affairs Select Committee, 2003). In conjunction with promoting water metering, the Government, in partnership with water companies, Ofwat and local authorities, should work to raise the profile of its assistance for low income and vulnerable householders who face difficulty paying their bill.

Improving water efficiency in new and existing homes

When the Sustainable Communities Plan was launched, the Deputy Prime Minister stated that water efficiency savings of between 20 and 30 per cent were crucial for new homes (Sustainable Buildings Task Group, 2004). There is currently no explicit requirement that Building Regulations should consider water efficiency, although they are under review. A 21 per cent reduction in pcc in new homes is achievable through the installation of affordable A-rated water saving household appliances and water efficient plumbing systems (WRSE Group, 2004). The Government should require that all new homes achieve a minimum of a 20 per cent reduction in pcc (based on national pcc) as part of Building Regulations.

The Government is currently developing with industry a voluntary Code for Sustainable Buildings. It should contain explicit requirements for water efficiency beyond that required in Building Regulations. The Code should recommend a 20 to 30 per cent reduction in pcc in new homes (based on average national pcc). Up to 25 per cent efficiency savings would be achievable without people changing the way they use water, through water efficient fixtures, fittings and new appliances. Water savings above 25 per cent would require changes to how people use water and may require changes in public attitudes towards the type of water they are using. For instance, rainwater harvesting requires people to water their gardens or wash their cars not from the tap, but from a water butt, which would be acceptable to many people. However, grey water recycling, which requires the re-use of some household water for low-water-quality applications, such as toilet flushing, is not currently popular. Encouraging grey water recycling at the household and community level will not only require overcoming the psychological hurdle of re-using water, but will require the fitting of reuse plumbing schemes, which will have a cost implication. As water reuse gains acceptability, it would be sensible to design new buildings to enable the incorporation of water reuse schemes.

Since 1996, water companies have had the duty to promote the efficient use of water by all their customers, which they have done with varying levels of success. Environmental and consumer groups have, however, long lamented the lack of a co-ordinated approach to water efficiency, and have called for some form of independent water saving trust, similar in structure to the Energy Saving Trust. In response, the Environment Agency has proposed to ministers an expanded and renamed Energy Saving Trust with a broader remit for providing information and grants to households on energy, transport, water and waste. This would benefit from economies of scale and be a 'one-stop shop'. Meanwhile, water companies have also recognised the need to take action and are planning to fund a new water saving body, although it is currently unclear what its objectives will be. There are clearly then a number of institutional and funding options for water efficiency.

A Water Efficiency Commitment for all homes

One potential concern regarding a Water Saving Body funded by water companies is that customers may not see it as independent and there may be a conflict of interest. On the one hand, water companies have a vested interest to sell more water, while on the other hand the purpose of a Water Saving Body would be to advocate less water use.

It will therefore be important that the proposed Water Saving Body operates within a policy framework that has clear targets for improving the water efficiency of new and existing homes. The Government could achieve this through the introduction of a water industry equivalent to the Energy Efficiency Commitment (EEC).

There are many lessons the water industry could take away from the EEC. The EEC is a levy on energy bills first introduced in 2002. Each supplier has an energy saving target that can be met by encouraging households to install energy saving measures. At least half the target must be met in households whose occupants are either on a low income or disabled. The EEC has successfully reduced energy use and carbon emissions and the Government's Energy Efficiency Action Plan has committed to extending the scheme to 2011 (Defra, 2004a). For an equivalent Water Efficiency Commitment, each water company should be set a water efficiency target with a requirement that a proportion of the target is met in low income and vulnerable households.

The Government spends, on average, £150 million per year on the Warm Front Scheme, which provides grants for heating and insulation to households. The scheme is central to the UK Fuel Poverty Strategy which has a target to eliminate fuel poverty in vulnerable groups by 2010 (DTI and Defra, 2001). In conjunction with a Water Efficiency Commitment, the Government would also need to provide grants to encourage low income, large households to adopt water efficiency measures.

The Water Efficiency Commitment need not be nationwide, but could be focused on regions with water stressed areas. Given the South East has high levels of household water use, the Government should encourage some of the South East water companies to participate in a regional pilot of the Water Efficiency Commitment. This would give South East water companies an opportunity to demonstrate their corporate commitment to water efficiency improvements and a head start in implementing the scheme. Ofwat could co-ordinate the pilot's implementation with guidance from the Government.

Flood risk in the South East

As with water resources, the Sustainable Communities Plan has been accused of understating the flood risk associated with new housing developments, raising questions, most notably from the Association of British Insurers (ABI), over the compatibility of the plan with policies to better manage and reduce flood risk. The Government is developing a new strategy for flooding and coastal erosion risk management called 'Making Space for Water' (Defra, 2004b) and has published some consultation responses (Defra, 2005b). Alongside the strategy, the Government is also reviewing Planning Policy Guidance (PPG) 25 on development and flood risk (ODPM, 2001). Significant parts of the growth areas in the South East are in the flood plain, but rather than seeking to ban development in these areas, the debate has shifted to how increased risk and social vulnerability can be minimised through planning, building design and flood risk reduction measures.

Understanding flood risk

Flooding is a natural process, vital for the maintenance of coastal and inland habitats. It cannot be eliminated, but can be managed to minimise the consequences. Flood risk is regarded as a combination of probability (how often an event is likely to occur) and consequences (the damage that would result from a flooding event).

The Environment Agency has produced a Flood Map that identifies areas at risk of river and coastal flooding across England and Wales according to three levels of flood probability as set out within PPG 25, alongside the appropriate planning response. For the ABI, developments located in areas where the annual probability of flooding is greater than 1.3 per cent (a 75 to one chance of flooding each year) are not guaranteed affordable insurance cover. The Government will consider relating indicative flood risk standards to the ABI's 1.3 per cent level of probability (Defra, 2005b).

When assessing flood risk, emphasis has been placed on probability, leading to the potential consequences of flooding not being adequately considered. This can lead to the mistaken belief that building behind existing defences does not increase risk, when the opposite is true, as risk increases as the potential scale of damage increases. This raises aggregate flood risk, presenting problems for re-insurance. The new PPS on flood risk and development will reflect the importance of taking account of the consequences, not just the probability of flooding events, and measures will be developed to take better account of environmental and social consequences as well as economic (Defra, 2005b).

Current and future flood risk

Nearly two million properties and five million people in the UK (roughly ten per cent) are potentially at risk from coastal or river flooding (Defra, 2004b). In the South East over 208,000 properties are located in the flood plain, but in an extreme flood event many more would be affected. The Flood Map does not currently include intra-urban or groundwater flooding. However, if scoping work shows it is feasible, these other sources of flooding will be incorporated during 2008-10 (Defra, 2005b). Across the UK, 80,000 properties are at risk in towns and cities from intra-urban flooding (Foresight, 2004) and as many as 380,000 properties on exposed chalk aquifers of Southern England may be vulnerable to groundwater flooding, which occurs when groundwater levels exceed the capacity of aquifers and water surfaces above ground (Defra, 2004c). Urbanisation, climate change and other risk factors will have a significant impact on the incidence and costs of flooding. Urbanisation (combined with climate change) will increase the risk of intra-urban flooding.

Economic impacts

The economic impact of flooding can be split into financial losses from flood events met through insurance and individual loss, and the economic costs of flood defences. The UK is unusual in having flood insurance as part of standard buildings insurance. In most industrialised countries, coverage for natural hazards, including flooding, involves some form of state support. Whether this arrangement can continue, as the impacts of climate change become more obvious, is uncertain and dependent on government providing and maintaining adequate defences, and ensuring that inappropriate development is kept off the flood plain.

In 2003-04 the total cost of flooding and managing flood risk in the UK was around £2.3 billion (Foresight, 2004). This equates to £800 million per annum spending on defences (split between £464 million for river and coastal defences and £320 million for intra-urban (including sewer) flooding) and annual flood damage costs averaging £1.4 billion (Foresight, 2004). In the South East, the value of assets at risk of flooding exceeds £50 billion, with the biggest threat coming from the sea and tidal waters

(Environment Agency, 2004a). Over the past five years, storm and flood losses have totalled £5 billion in the UK, more than 60 per cent up on previous years (ABI, 2004).

The Exchequer currently provides nearly all the funding for flood risk management and raised funding of the flood defence programme in England and Wales, to a record £564 million per year for 2005-06. The Government has stated that this high level is to be maintained over each of the three years of the Spending Review 2004 period to 2007-08 (HM Treasury, 2004).

The Foresight report (2004) examined the effects of different greenhouse gas emission scenarios on future flood risk. If flood risk management policies and expenditure remained unchanged, annual losses would increase under every scenario by the 2080s. But the variation in the costs is wide ranging, from less than £1 billion under the Local Stewardship scenario (low-medium emissions) to around £27 billion under World Markets (high emissions). Figure 7 shows that for most of the emissions scenarios, the South East would experience the highest annual damage to residential and commercial developments compared to the other English regions and Wales. This is partly because the effects of climate change are expected to be the worst in the South East compared to other parts of the country (UKCIP, 2002).

Figure 7: Expected annual damage to residential and commercial developments across the English regions and Wales (£m), 2000 and 2080s. (Assuming flood management approach and expenditure remain unchanged.)

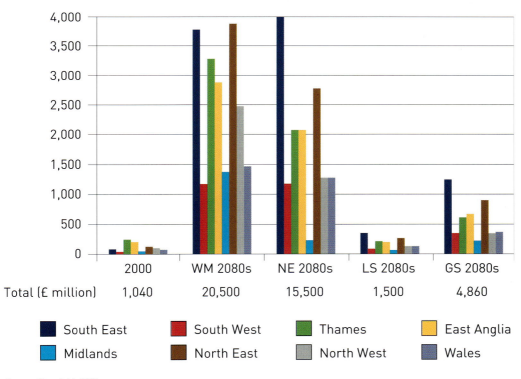

Source: Foresight, 2004

Human impacts

Beyond economic costs, flooding has other human impacts including loss of life, health hazards and emotional distress. While statistics do a poor job of gauging social impacts, in terms of numbers, it is expected that by the 2080s the numbers at risk from both river and coastal flooding and intra-urban flooding will be substantially higher than the five million at risk currently (Foresight, 2004). While the number of people at risk from river and coastal flooding in the South East will be higher than today, it will be much lower than the number at risk in London and East Anglia.

It is debatable whether any particular section of the population has an increased likelihood of exposure to flooding. While people in the lowest income deciles did not disproportionately reside within the flood plains of rivers in England, there appeared to be some correlation between people living in the most deprived wards and proximity to tidal flood plains (Walker et al., 2003). Some groups are more vulnerable to flood events than others. Vulnerability can be considered as exposure to a given risk and the ability to cope (resilience). There is substantial evidence that the elderly, disabled and less affluent are more vulnerable to flood impacts because they find it difficult to cope and recover after a flood event (Walker et al., 2003). Poorer people are also less likely to be insured and therefore less likely to be able to recover all their lost assets or rebuild their damaged homes, with the consequent physical and psychological stress involved (Enarson and Fordham, 2001).

Flood risk in the South East growth areas

A recent report for the ABI assessed the costs of flooding in the growth areas and evaluated various different options to reduce flood risk (ABI, 2005). This section reports on some of its key findings for the South East growth areas, as outlined in the Sustainable Communities Plan (ODPM, 2003). It should be noted that this report only considered economic risks. While recognising the interests of the insurance industry on economic risk, it would be helpful if the debate on flood risk in the growth areas considered the social and environmental consequences of building in flood risk areas.

As Table 5 shows, 15 per cent of existing development in all the growth areas is currently in the flood plain. Of the development planned for 2016-2021, 30 per cent has been allocated in flood risk areas where the annual probability of flooding is between 0.1 and 1.3 per cent (between a 1,000 to one and 75 to one chance of flooding).

Table 5: Existing and proposed development in the flood plain – for all the growth areas and in the South East growth areas

	Development currently in flood plain (%)	New development in flood plain 2016-2021 (%)	New development in significant flood risk areas 2016-21 (>1.3% or 75:1) annual probability
All growth areas	15	30	10
Ashford	8	7	0
Aylesbury	8	19	11
Milton Keynes	2	2	0
Kent Thameside	7	45	8
North Kent	11	65	Unknown

Source: Compiled from information in ABI, 2005

The South East parts of the Thames Gateway growth areas have higher percentages (65 per cent in North Kent and 45 per cent in Kent Thameside) of developments in flood plains compared to Ashford, Milton Keynes and Aylesbury. Of more concern are the developments that are planned for flood risk areas where the annual probability of flooding is greater than 1.3 per cent (greater than a 75 to one chance of flooding). Between 2016 and 2021, Aylesbury and Kent Thameside are planning to put around 10 per cent of new development in the significant flood risk areas.

In Milton Keynes and Ashford 30 per cent of flood defences do not provide a 1.3 per cent (75-year) standard of protection (ABI, 2005). However, many parts of Milton Keynes are naturally protected due to land elevation, or have adjacent land with relatively low asset value such as open space, and so the proportion of defences with a low standard of defence will not necessarily present a problem to new developments. Ashford is more susceptible to flooding. In the parts of Ashford that have experienced flooding in recent years there has been investment in defences, and Ashford's defences are regarded as generally good (ABI, 2005), but it is recognised that present defences will require review. This is being conducted as part of the 'Ashford's Future' work.

In Aylesbury more than three quarters of its defences do not offer the 1.3 per cent (75-year) standard of protection. This is of potential concern as there is a high risk of flooding in parts of Aylesbury. If Aylesbury is to accommodate new development in the flood plain, then measures will need to be provided to offset any increase in flood risk.

The Thames Barrier is part of a major system of flood defence measures designed to protect London from a 0.1 per cent annual flood (1,000-year flood event). The Thames Gateway growth areas, and areas such as East London and South Essex, therefore currently have high standards of protection of between 0.5 and 0.1 per cent (between a 200-year and 1,000-year standard of protection). The current barrier is expected to provide a high standard of defence up until about 2030 allowing for sea level rises. 'Thames 2100' is the Environment Agency sub-group taking forward plans for ensuring the Thames Gateway growth areas and other parts of London continue to be protected from flooding to that standard beyond 2030.

Across all the growth areas, flood management measures will need to be periodically reviewed to ensure a high standard of protection. If no steps are taken, the ABI (2005) estimates that the proposed developments (in all growth areas) between 2016 and 2021 could increase the financial costs of fluvial and coastal flooding by an average of £54.6 million – a 74 per cent increase in potential flood damages within the growth areas and a five per cent increase in national flood risk. Consequential flood losses (infrastructure damage and business interruption costs) could add between £19 million and £27 million per year to this total. The losses from intra-urban flood sources could increase losses by another £14.6 million. The majority of this extra cost comes from new development in the Thames Gateway, accounting for £47.1 million a year, compared to £7.5 million for all the other growth areas combined. The South East's share of these costs would be relatively small.

Managing flood risk in the South East

In examining what the nation's aims should be for future flood risk management, the Foresight report (2004) offered a blunt option: should we accept increasing levels of flooding, seek to maintain existing risk-levels, or seek to reduce the risks of flooding? The first would have undesirable social as well as economic consequences, and goes against a trend in society that expects increasing safety standards and risk reduction. This trend also suggests the second option may be undesirable. The third option would require considerable additional investment in flood risk management, but the economic benefits of this would be significantly greater than the economic costs (Foresight, 2004).

Risk reduction needs to be approached from a broader front than just looking at new development, for example through rural land use, and emergency responses. However, this section discusses how new development can proceed in a way that minimises flood risk. There are pro-active steps that the Government, local authorities and developers can take in this area, and Table 6 shows some of the options for mitigating flood risk for new developments in the growth areas.

Table 6: Options for mitigating flood risk (for new developments)

Option	Comment (applicability to different growth areas)	Climate proofed
Moving property off the flood plain	Policy potentially very successful in Ashford, M11 and South Midlands growth areas but limited in Thames Gateway.	Yes
Moving property to lower risk sites	Policy potentially successful in all growth areas but could be limited in some areas by land supply.	No – as some lower risk sites could increase in risk with climate change
Reducing vulnerability – reduced ground floor living (residential property only)	Most suited to homes located in significant risk areas.	Yes, but flooding still inconvenient
Reducing vulnerability – flood resilience (residential property only)	Most suited to homes located in significant risk areas.	Yes, but flooding still inconvenient
Flood alleviation – defence improvements	Traditional approach to flood mitigation but important issues of long term maintenance costs and the implications of climate change.	No – climate change needs to be explicitly factored into defence design
Flood alleviation – land raising	Complete flood avoidance but could have negative effect upon nearby existing development.	No – elevation cannot be increased after initial development
Flood alleviation – flood storage	Successful in some areas but requires large land areas.	Yes
Flood alleviation – Sustainable Drainage Systems (SuDS)	Should be adopted in all new development to mitigate intra-urban flood problems (see later section on SuDS)	Yes (potentially)

Source: ABI, 2005

Mitigating climate change

Reducing global greenhouse gas emissions would substantially help to manage both future flood risk and water shortages. In the absence of other responses, if the world emitted low emissions rather than high emissions in a high growth scenario, the risks of catchment and coastal flooding would fall from around £21 billion per year to around £15 billion per year in the 2080s. In the case of intra-urban flooding, mitigating climate change could make the difference between the existing system of drains and sewers coping, or reaching the limit of their capacity (Foresight, 2004). However, action to reduce greenhouse gas emissions needs to be achieved at a global level. Under the Kyoto Protocol, the UK has committed to reducing greenhouse gas emissions by 12.5 per cent by 2010 and the Government's intention is to move towards a 60 per cent reduction in carbon emissions by 2050 (DTI/Defra, 2004).

Avoiding building in the flood plain through land use planning

The planning system plays a key role in controlling the location, density and design of new development. Not building in the flood plain is an obvious way to reduce flood risk both to new development and to other properties whose risk may be increased through building on the flood plain (ABI, 2005). Effective land-use planning to manage flood risk could reduce the aggregate cost of flood defences from £52 billion to £22 billion until the 2080s (Foresight, 2004). In the growth areas, if properties were moved off the flood plain and housing densities increased in non-flood risk locations, then flood risk could be reduced by 89-96 per cent for all growth areas except Thames Gateway (ABI, 2005) and by 79-86 per cent in Ashford (ABI, 2005).

Despite PPG 25 directing development away from flood plain areas, and a high level target (HLT 12) to prevent all new inappropriate development in flood plains by 2007, development is still occurring in flood plain areas against Environment Agency advice. There was initial progress when the number of planning applications approved against Environment Agency advice decreased from 37 per cent in 2001-02 to 21 per cent in 2002-03, but there was a slight rise to 22.5 per cent in 2003-04 (Environment Agency, 2005b).

The Government has indicated its willingness to tackle this problem (Defra, 2005b). The ODPM will be consulting on whether to make the Environment Agency a statutory consultee in relation to planning applications in areas of flood risk. It will also be considering whether to give the Government greater powers to call in developments that are permitted against the sustained objection of the Environment Agency, for determination by the Secretary of State (Defra, 2005b). This review process would need to be transparent and accountable, particularly in areas like the Thames Gateway, which are politically sensitive.

In some cases, the Government's target for 60 per cent of new build to be on brownfield land (in PPG 3) can conflict with its advice to direct new development away from flood risk areas (in PPG 25). Following historical land-use patterns, brownfield land tends to be located in the flood plain. However, there is no publicly available information on how much brownfield land is on or off the flood plain in the South East, or if brownfield land off the flood plain is reaching capacity. What we do know is that the South East region is exceeding the brownfield target, reaching 62 per cent in 2003 (ODPM, 2005), and that it has achieved this with an average of ten per cent of new dwellings built in flood risk areas between 1999 and 2002, slightly below the England average of 11 per cent (ODPM, 2004). A problem for planners and developers is that PPG 25 is unclear over the relative priority of each policy, although this may be clarified in the new PPS on development and flood risk (Defra, 2005b).

Strategic flood risk assessments are an essential part of ensuring that flood risk is considered in development planning but are not currently required for RSSs or LDFs leaving flood risk to be considered on a case-by-case basis. The Government has indicated that it will strongly encourage the inclusion of strategic flood risk assessments to inform RSSs and LDFs (Defra, 2005b). Similarly, sewerage and drainage capacity is not currently considered at a strategic level by local authorities and there is confusion over co-ordination and responsibility. The Government is proposing to take forward the concept of integrated urban drainage management and will pilot a range of different approaches from 2006 (Defra, 2005b).

Although water companies and the Environment Agency are consulted on planning applications, drainage issues can arise after initial planning permission is granted. It would make more sense to make drainage a material consideration that is factored in at the start of the planning application process. Better incorporating (and acting upon) flood risk assessments and the consideration of water resources, sewerage and drainage capacity into the planning process would have implications for both local and regional planners. They may require additional training, supplementary planning guidance and perhaps more time – so that they can account for these issues when assessing planning applications and strategies.

Reducing the vulnerability of buildings through design

Developments at risk of flooding can be designed to be more flood resilient, by, for example moving living space above the likely level of flooding. Alternatively the ground floor can be kept as living space, but made more flood resilient through concrete floors and wiring electrics above the likely flood level. Such measures may be included in revised Building Regulations in 2009 (Defra, 2005b) but could also be included in the Code for Sustainable Building. Although these measures are regarded as 'climate proof' by the ABI, flood impacts will still be a nuisance and pose a risk to people. Reducing the vulnerability of building has cost implications. The construction of an extra storey typically increases building costs by 25-30 per cent (ABI, 2005) and making a property more resilient could increase costs by 12-15 per cent. However many flood resilient measures will pay for themselves in areas prone to frequent flooding (ABI, 2005).

Reducing flood risk through flood alleviation schemes

Flood risk can be further reduced through flood alleviation measures. These include flood defences, land raising, flood storage and/or Sustainable Drainage Systems (SuDS). Table 6 shows how these options may or may not be suitable for the growth areas. The Government is moving away from the provision of traditional flood defences, towards a catchment approach that uses appropriate and cost-effective measures that minimise flood risk while enhancing biodiversity and the landscape (Environment Agency, 2004a). This includes a greater emphasis on flood storage and SuDS, so rather than constraining and directing water out of the catchment as quickly as possible, flood waters are recognised as a resource that need to feed back into the catchment and replenish water resources. This is of obvious importance in many areas of the South East that are already water stressed.

SuDS are designed to manage surface water run-off to both attenuate the run-off and provide varying degrees of water treatment through filtration etc. SuDS schemes vary considerably and costs depend on the site size and the nature of run-off. Defra, the

Environment Agency and the ODPM all advocate SuDS as the recommended approach to surface drainage, and PPG 25 encourages use of SuDS wherever possible in new developments. SuDS should be a mandatory consideration in all new developments, and if impracticable, effort should be made in the local catchment to compensate for the extra surface water run-off. Appropriate legislative and policy changes are needed to ensure their widespread use and proper management, and these are being considered as part of the Government's Making Space for Water consultation (Defra, 2005).

Paying for protection

Many of the UK's flood defences need maintaining, upgrading, replacing, or in some circumstances, abandoning. Although developers are responsible for fully funding the provision and future maintenance of any new flood risk reduction measures necessary for developments in flood risk areas, it is unclear exactly how much developers have contributed to flood defences. Therefore, the Government may be called on to subsidise flood alleviation and flood resilience measures that may be needed for new developments. The Government has been considering how additional funds could be raised and is looking at implementing a flood development connection charge in recognition of the benefits that developments might get from existing flood risk management services (Defra, 2004b).

If planning regulations do not guide development off the flood plain and/or funding for flood risk management is inadequate, there may be pressure for insurance to more strongly reflect the logic of the market, to steer development away from the floodplain. This may make insurance unaffordable to some households, and put pressure on the Government to become the 'insurer of last resort'. If this were to happen, and it is not an outcome currently given serious thought by the insurance industry, this would mean taxpayers paying for damages to the individual, when they currently assume that risk themselves. This would be unacceptable, and it is imperative that planning regulations on development and flood risk are adhered to by all authorities and that the Government continues to fund flood risk management adequately.

Key findings

Is there enough water to meet the rising demand for new housing and domestic consumption in the South East?

There is potentially enough water in the South East to meet the rising demand for new housing and domestic consumption, *but only* with high water efficiency savings in existing and new homes and the timely provision of new water resources. Relying only on supply-side measures, such as new or enlarged reservoirs, to meet increasing demand would be a risky strategy. Even with these measures, there are some areas in the South East with severe water stress or fragile water quality, where further significant development should be limited or avoided.

Reducing leakage

- The Office of Water Services (Ofwat) should more rigorously enforce leakage targets and there should be clear penalties for water companies who consistently fail to meet their target.

Increasing water efficiency

- The Government, water companies and Ofwat should consider how to speed up the installation of meters in areas of low water availability and accompany this with a high profile awareness raising campaign on water efficiency.

- The Environment Agency should be given a stronger role to independently assess when supply zones should be declared as Water Scarce Areas.

- The profile of government assistance for low income and vulnerable householders who face difficulties paying their water bill must be raised.

- Building Regulations should require that all new homes meet a minimum of a 20 per cent reduction in per capita consumption (pcc) of water (compared to the national average).

- The Code for Sustainable Buildings should recommend a 20 to 30 per cent reduction in pcc of water (compared to the national average) in new homes. Achieving water efficiency savings above 25 per cent will require changes to the way people use water and will need public acceptance.

- The Government should consider introducing a water industry counterpart to the Energy Efficiency Commitment (EEC) for improving the water efficiency of new and existing homes. Each water company should be set a water saving target, with a proportion of the target to be met in low income, larger households.

- The South East should participate in a regional pilot of a Water Efficiency Commitment.

Co-ordinating water resource management and development planning

- Both the availability of water resources and water quality, over the lifetime of the development, should be material considerations in development planning.

- Development plans should be developed in tandem with water resource plans, and both should consider long-term climate change impacts.

- Water companies should become statutory consultees for Regional Spatial Strategies (RSSs) and Local Development Frameworks (LDFs).

What impact will new housing developments have on flood risk in the South East growth areas?

Across the growth areas, 15 per cent of existing development is currently in the flood-plain. Of the new development planned for 2016-21, 30 per cent of the allocated sites will be in flood risk areas. However, the majority of these sites will be in areas where the annual probability of flooding is either low or moderate. Across all the growth areas, flood management measures will need to be periodically reviewed to ensure a high standard of protection. The Association of British Insurers (ABI) has identified a sequential approach to minimising flood risk through careful planning, the design of more resilient buildings and appropriate flood protection. It is imperative that this approach is followed for all new development in the growth areas.

Managing flood risk

- RSSs and LDFs should include a strategic flood risk assessment.

- The Environment Agency should be statutory consultee on all new developments in flood risk locations.

- The Secretary of State with oversight for planning should review developments permitted against the sustained objection of the Environment Agency, through a transparent and accountable review process.

- The risk of sewer flooding, and sewer and drainage capacity should become a material planning consideration.

6. The Commission's key findings: cross cutting themes

The South East is already, and is likely to remain, one of Europe's most prosperous regions. The challenge facing the South East is how it can maintain its economic success whilst enhancing its environment and improving the wellbeing and quality of life of all its citizens. There are five cross cutting themes that summarise the Commission's findings and how the South East can address this challenge:

1. The South East's inter-relationship with London, the rest of the UK and Europe;

2. Addressing disparities within the South East;

3. Developing incentives for sustainable choices;

4. Meeting infrastructure needs;

5. Improving governance and planning arrangements.

1. The South East's inter-relationship with London, the rest of the UK and Europe

Central to the Commission's goal was to '... take into account the position of the South East with regards to London as a world city and as the frontier to mainland Europe, as well as considering the UK's inter-regional disparities.' The South East is not only one of the most prosperous regions in the UK, it is also one of the most prosperous regions in the EU. The economic performance of the South East compares well with what are generally regarded as the EU's most prosperous substantive regions containing all the well known centres of commerce in Europe outside of London and Paris (see table 2 in chapter 2).

The *South East Plan: Consultation Draft* proposes a three per cent growth rate per annum in output – or Gross Value Added (GVA) (SEERA, 2005) which is in line with the Regional Economic Strategy (SEEDA, 2002). There is broad consensus in the South East for continued economic growth in the region at about current levels. No-one in the region appears to be arguing for an *increased* rate of economic growth in the South East.

The South East has a close relationship with London both in terms of its economy and housing market. About 11 per cent of those in employment in the South East commute into London to work and as result about six per cent of the economic output of London is derived from South East commuters (LSE/Corporation of London, 2003). This has led to debates about whether it is the labour of the South East that helps to drive the London economy, or whether it is the buoyancy of the London economy that provides jobs for people living in the South East. It is probably pointless to have this debate, as in economic and labour market terms there is little difference between someone who works and lives in London and someone who works in London but lives in a South East commuter town.

London and the East of England are the only regions that make net contributions to the population of the South East, although London is by far the largest contributor. In 2002-03, the South East received nearly a third of all migrants leaving London (ONS, 2003). This pattern is heavily influenced by international migration. London is the dominant destination for international migrants – about 70 per cent of the total net inflow into the UK (ONS, 2003). The South East's share of international migrants is modest. It is, however, indirectly affected by London's attraction of migrants, which adds pressure to the housing market in the capital that then results in an out-migration 'cascade effect', increasing population pressures in the South East.

While we know much about the South East's inter-relationship with London, there are still many issues we are unclear about. International migration trends are notoriously hard to forecast. As a consequence, predicting the impact that future international migration could have on housing demand in the capital, and thereby in the South East, is very difficult. However, there are other relationships between housing demand in the capital and the surrounding regions that are also important. Many people move in and out of the capital at certain points in their lives to meet their aspirations for different forms of housing. Those people moving out of London into the South East tend to be families and older people. Nonetheless, the link between international migration into London and population pressures in the South East does present a difficult political issue.

The projected annual household growth in London, over the period 2001-2011, could be as high as 48,300 (ODPM, 2004a). Housebuilding in London has only averaged 15,000 over the last decade, with current provision at 23,920 (ODPM, 2005), which suggests that meeting the capital's housing needs will be challenging, although recent trends in housing completions are more favourable. A debate needs to be had about whether neighbouring regions like the South East can be expected to fill the gap if London is unable to meet its own housing needs. London also has to address how it will accommodate a greater population, probably at higher densities.

Another unclear issue is how much of London's water demand is met from water resources in the South East. London currently relies on reservoirs in the South East for some of its water. The water demands that will result from additional housing growth in London have not been factored into the *South East Plan: Consultation Draft* (WRSE Group, 2004 and 2005). It is therefore unknown what impact this could have on water availability and the capacity of sewerage and drainage systems in the South East.

There are a number of clear comparisons which can be drawn with the South East and the rest of the UK. While England as whole has been experiencing fairly strong population growth in recent years, most of this growth has been concentrated in the regions of the Greater South East. Between 2003 and 2028, the South East is projected to have the fastest growing population of any region in England (ODPM, 2004a).

The South East's travel patterns are not greatly different compared to the other English regions. Between 1992-94 and 2003, people in the South East made slightly more trips and travelled slightly longer distances compared to their counterparts in the other English regions. Their journey purposes were broadly similar to people in the rest of Great Britain, with the majority being for leisure purposes (NTS, 1985-86 to 2003). What distinguishes the South East is its high dependence on the car. The South East has high levels of car ownership and motorists in the South East drive more miles by car compared to most other English regions (NTS, 2003). This is in part a function of the relative affluence of the region, but also because of deficiencies in public transport particularly intra-regional transport links. As a consequence, greenhouse gas emissions from private vehicles per household are higher in the South East than the UK average (ONS, 2004).

Households in the South East consume more water per capita compared to most other regions, yet the South East has some of the lowest water metering rates in England and Wales (Environment Agency, 2004). In the longer term, the risks associated with flooding will be affected by levels of greenhouse gas emissions. The effects of climate change are forecast to be worse in the South East compared to other parts of the UK (UKCIP, 2002). Compared to the other English regions, the South East could experience the highest annual damage to residential and commercial developments from flooding over future decades (Foresight, 2004).

The South East is the only UK region with an above average growth rate in output per head (EBS, 2004). In contrast the North East and Wales are the two UK regions with a below average growth rate. Despite the Government having a target to reduce disparities between regions, it has acknowledged that inter-regional disparities are in fact getting worse (ODPM, 2005).

The determination within government to address regional disparities in economic performance and to address low levels of employment, would be best served by reformulating the Public Service Agreement (PSA) target that relates to regional economic performance. A suggested alternative for the 2006 Spending Review would be:

> Over the long term reduce the persistent gap in output per head between the UK's regions by concentrating effort on increasing the growth rate in the lagging regions (with a particular focus on employment).

For the South East region this would mean voicing support for the efforts of the less prosperous regions, individually and collectively, to tackle their economic problems and particularly their relatively low employment rates. The emphasis here is not on what could be characterised as old fashioned policy instruments, designed to move economic activity around the country, but policies to improve employment and skills within the less prosperous regions.

The South East has a strong interest in encouraging the Government to boost the economic performance of the less prosperous regions in the UK. This would help ease the pressures on the region that have been generated by the relative shift in economic activity and population to the Greater South East. This in turn would make it easier for the South East to cope with the problems that current levels of relative economic prosperity pose including traffic congestion, lack of affordable housing, the unsustainable use of natural resources and the degradation of the natural environment. In doing so, the region could focus on developing a new approach to growth driven by quality of life priorities that encourages the transition to a low carbon economy.

2. Addressing disparities within the South East

Although the South East is one of the most prosperous regions in the UK and EU, there are serious economic disparities within the region especially along parts of the south coast. There are also low employment rates amongst disadvantaged groups such as the long term sick and disabled. Tackling economic inactivity and increasing employment rates is not only important for reducing disparities between regions, it is also key to narrowing disparities within the South East. This is something the Government has come to recognise, although agencies and authorities in the South East appear to be still catching up with this shift in national policy focus.

Even in a region with a relatively good overall employment rate there is still plenty of scope for increasing employment in those parts of the South East, such as Thanet, where employment rates are more comparable with the labour markets of the less prosperous northern regions. The Government has a target for an 80 per cent employment rate for all adults aged 16-64 by around 2020 (DWP, 2005). In the South East the current overall employment rate is 77 per cent. Meeting the Government's target will require specific attention to be given to increasing the labour market participation of the economically inactive.

Raising employment rates could have important implications for the demand for new housing within the South East. There are those within the South East who argue that without a significantly higher level of housing growth, it will be difficult to accommodate extra people moving into the region, which would result in labour shortfalls. They argue that this in turn would have negative ramifications for the economic performance of the region.

There are two counter-arguments to this view. The first is that, while the labour market in the South East is relatively tight it is not overheating. Skills shortages and skills gaps do not seem to be a bigger problem in the South East than in other English regions and are not getting worse (National Employer Skills Survey, LSC, 2003). The shortages that do exist are surprisingly widely spread across both higher and lower skilled occupations.

Second, if the South East significantly raised employment rates within the region there would be less need for higher levels of in-migration, which would have implications for the rate of housing growth required. Over the last decade, the average annual rate of housebuilding in the South East has been 24,400. The *South East Plan: Consultation Draft* is examining future annual housing growth rates that are all higher than 24,300. The range of options under consideration is: 25,500, 28,000 and 32,000 (SEERA, 2005).

Research commissioned by the South East England Development Agency (SEEDA) shows that reducing the number of economically inactive by 265,000 over the lifetime of the South East Plan (which looks out to 2026) would mean that the labour shortfalls resulting from a range of housing growth rates could be much lower than expected. At an annual housing growth rate of 32,000 (the highest option in the *South East Plan: Consultation Draft*) the labour shortfall suggested by the work of Deloitte for SEEDA would be just 46,000. For an annual housing growth rate of 28,000 (the middle range in the *South East Plan: Consultation Draft*) the labour shortfall would be 113,000 (SEEDA, 2005). Neither of these shortfalls would make a significant difference to the South East's economy. For the 28,000 annual housing growth rate the projected labour shortfall would result in the rate of economic growth falling from three per cent to 2.9 per cent per year. Furthermore, this research did not account for the impact of an increase in the employment rates of women aged 59-64 in the South East, as a result of the state pension age rising between 2010 and 2020, which would reduce these labour shortfalls still further.

The South East is already able to draw on the most highly qualified labour from national and, indeed, international markets. Improvements in skills attainment within the region will also help meet the demand for more highly qualified labour. There needs to be a balance between in-migration and mobilising the labour supply within the region to meet future labour demand. The challenge facing the South East is to increase employment rates in its less prosperous areas and among older workers and groups disadvantaged in the labour market. If it can meet this challenge, significantly higher levels of housing growth – above those set out in the *South East Plan: Consultation Draft* – cannot be justified on the basis that otherwise there would be significant negative implications for the South East's economy.

But a somewhat higher level of housing growth in the South East could be justified on the grounds of meeting affordable housing needs. The South East is the second least affordable region in the UK for first time buyers. There are also rising numbers of people living in temporary accommodation in the region. The priority for the South East is to secure more affordable housing (both socially rented and intermediate) for those people already living within the region.

While the Barker Review's (2004) consideration of affordable housing needs was welcome, there are reservations about the underlying methodology supporting its recommendations. It is unclear whether it is possible for policy-makers to set targets for output in the housing market to achieve a particular path for house price inflation. The Barker Review came up with a national headline figure of an extra 141,000 dwellings per year to reduce real house price inflation to 1.1 per cent per annum (Barker, 2004). Research commissioned by ippr suggested that if only about half that figure were built nationally it would have a similar effect on house price inflation (Bramley, 2005). This raises question marks over the robustness of the Barker methodology and the extent to which it can be relied upon to develop both national and regional affordability targets, which the Government is current developing. To meet affordability problems in the South East a direct increase in the provision of affordable housing would seem to be the most appropriate policy response.

It is important to get the right mix between private sector housebuilding and the provision of various types of affordable housing, to help create sustainable communities. This will not be achieved with levels of housebuilding lower than those proposed in the *South East Plan: Consultation Draft*. Levels of housebuilding above those options in the *South East Plan: Consultation Draft* would not be politically acceptable within the region.

The objective in the *South East Plan: Consultation Draft* is for 25 per cent of all extra housing to be social and another 10-15 per cent intermediate (SEERA, 2005). At a growth rate of 32,000, this would imply about 12,000 affordable homes a year and about 20,000 homes built without public subsidy (private sector homes). In the past decade the private sector has been delivering at about this level. At a growth rate of 28,000, if the same proportion of affordable homes were built (equating to about 10,500) then private housebuilding rates would need to fall, which would not seem likely to fit the aspirations of people in a relatively affluent region. Alternatively, if past private house-building rates were maintained, the proportion of affordable housing would need to fall to a little more than a quarter of the total. This would mean the affordable housing targets set out in the *South East Plan: Consultation Draft* would not be met.

It is also important to consider housing's role in supporting local regeneration. Simply building new housing in less prosperous areas will not per se deliver regeneration. There are other related policy levers that need attention if the South East is to be effective at raising employment rates, particularly in less prosperous areas. For instance, the restricted accessibility of residents in the coastal towns to available employment opportunities has been exacerbated by poor quality public transport, especially intra-regional links (GOSE, 2002). The *South East Plan: Consultation Draft* identifies a number of key locations for the movement of people and goods within the region called 'transport hubs' (SEERA, 2005). These transport hubs are business and service centres that could be classified as prosperous areas and/or areas of strong economic potential. Improving the quality of existing local bus and rail services could make it easier for people in the coastal towns to reach potential employment opportunities in transport hubs such as Ashford. The South East needs to take an approach to local regeneration that considers housing, transport and employment policies in an integrated way.

3. Developing incentives for sustainable choices

If the South East is to maintain its current rate of economic growth and offer its citizens a high quality of life, it will need to develop policy measures that influence the attitudes and behaviour of individuals and firms. The Government, South East authorities and agencies, firms and individuals need to take collective responsibility for improving quality of life in the South East. The challenge facing policy-makers is to identify policy options that encourage and enable individuals and firms to consume resources more efficiently and produce less waste and pollution. Part of this will involve developing new ways of paying for services to encourage more sustainable consumption choices through, for example, road user charging and water metering. Alongside this, meeting the associated infrastructure requirements will also be critical.

Residents in the South East cite increases in traffic congestion and pollution as two of their top local priorities (MORI, 2004). However, there are no signs of these quality of life pressures abating. By 2010, road traffic is expected to grow by between 23 and 29 per cent across England (DfT, 2005a) and by 25 per cent in the South East (see chapter 4) from 2000 levels. Road transport already accounts for 20 per cent of the UK's total carbon emissions (DfT, 2005a). There is a growing recognition among politicians and the public that we cannot build our way out of our traffic congestion problems.

The UK and congested regions like the South East are facing a tough choice, between increasing traffic delays and pollution or bold measures for managing traffic growth and investing in public transport options. The success of the Central London congestion charge has undoubtedly helped to build political momentum for the use of price signals in influencing travel behaviour and reducing demand for road transport. Maintaining this momentum will require significant upfront investment in transport infrastructure before a national congestion charging scheme can be introduced. Over the longer term the South East should encourage the Government to press ahead with plans to introduce a national congestion charging scheme within the next ten years. A national congestion charging scheme, introduced on a revenue raising basis (on top of existing motoring taxes), could help to reduce the rate of traffic growth in the South East by nine per cent by 2010 (see chapter 4).

There are also short to medium term pathways for cutting congestion, such as local urban charging schemes and motorway tolling. While many, including the Government, view local urban charging schemes as an effective tool for tackling congestion in the short term and as a useful step towards a national scheme, some local authorities and local people still have serious reservations. Ultimately it is up to local communities and not central government to decide whether an urban charging scheme is the best way to manage traffic demand in a local area.

If the Government wants to see local urban charging being progressed in the South East and elsewhere, it will need to provide local authorities with funding for packages of measures that combine road pricing with local public transport improvements. Alongside this, local authorities should gain greater control over local bus services through quality contracts which regulate routes, fares and timetables. The South East should also explore options for introducing motorway tolling on congested commuter routes as well as tolling on major motorway sections that are due to be widened, to help ease congestion on busy commuter routes. Motorway tolling schemes could be introduced as public-private partnerships, whereby the financial risks, administration and revenue are shared with the private sector.

Smarter travel measures could also help to cut congestion while encouraging public transport use, cycling or walking in the South East and across the UK. Options such as personalised travel planning, public transport marketing, travel plans and car clubs focus on improving information about travel choices rather than altering the regulatory or charging framework within which travel choices are made. They tend to be most effective when combined with harder edged, demand management measures. There is considerable potential for scaling up smarter travel measures, and case study evidence suggests that they could have a significant impact on reducing car trips (DfT, 2004a). Given a revenue raising national congestion charge could only reduce the rate at which traffic is set to increase, the potential for smarter travel measures cannot be neglected.

Only with significant water efficiency savings in existing and new homes and the timely provision of new water resources will there potentially be enough water to meet rising demand for new housing and domestic consumption in the region. Households make up over half of public water use in the South East (Environment Agency, 2001). As with road transport, this will require a new way of paying for water use. Most customers in England and Wales currently pay a fixed rate for their water which is not related to how much they use. Water metering can help to change people's attitudes to water use and encourage them to save water and money by using water efficient appliances and measures in their homes. Higher levels of water metering should be encouraged in areas of low water availability in the South East. Some organisations have voiced concerns that metering could potentially result in poorer households sacrificing hygiene to save money (Fitch and Price, 2002). But recent research suggests that water metering would in fact be progressive from the point of view of low income households (Ekins and Dresner, 2004).

In addition to water metering, there should be tougher regulations placed on developers to improve the water efficiency of new buildings. The Government should require that all new homes achieve at least a 20 per cent reduction in per capita consumption (pcc) as part of the Building Regulations. The Government is currently developing with industry a voluntary Code for Sustainable Buildings to promote resource efficient buildings that use less water and energy and create less waste (Defra, 2005a). The code should be applied across the Greater South East growth areas.

In addition to developers, water companies also have a major role to play in reducing water leakage and encouraging greater water efficiency. The water companies are planning to fund a new water saving body to provide advice and incentives to households as well as businesses to adopt water saving measures. It will be important that the proposed Water Saving Body operates within a policy framework that has clear targets for benchmarking water saving improvements. The Government should introduce a water industry equivalent to the Energy Efficiency Commitment (EEC). Each water company could be set water efficiency targets for reducing levels of water consumption in both households and businesses. The Water Efficiency Commitment need not be nationwide but could be focused on regions with water stressed areas. Given the South East has high levels of household water use, the Government should encourage some of the South East water companies to participate in a regional pilot of the Water Efficiency Commitment.

The effects of water shortages and flooding in the South East will almost certainly intensify over future decades with climate change and increased development. The Government and other public agencies need to raise public awareness of the longer term risks of more frequent water shortages or flooding, so that people can make informed choices about to what extent they are willing to accept these future risks. It is unclear whether people would put more pressure on public agencies to alter their approaches to development and/or strengthen flood defences and flood warning mechanisms if they had a better awareness of these longer term risks.

4. Meeting infrastructure needs

The UK needs an open debate about whether, as a nation, we are prepared to devote the resources necessary to deliver a range of housing policy objectives, including the Government's Sustainable Communities Plan (ODPM, 2003) and to meet other associated demands for improved infrastructure in areas such as transport and flood defences.

There has been a legacy of under-spending on housing and transport in the UK. Figure 1 shows that both housing and transport saw sharp declines in public spending as a proportion of Gross Domestic Product (GDP) from the early 1990s and through the first three to four years of this Labour government. It is challenging to believe that the Government will genuinely be able to deliver sustainable communities with public spending on housing at two-thirds of the level of national income that was being devoted in the early 1990s and transport spending also lower as a proportion of national income.

The Government has dedicated extra public resources to delivering its sustainable communities agenda. The 2004 Spending Review included a commitment to fund an extra 10,000 social homes a year by 2008 (a 50 per cent increase in provision) and established a £200 million Community Infrastructure Fund (CIF) for transport investment (HMT, 2004).

Figure 1: Public spending on transport and housing as a percentage of GDP, 1989-2008

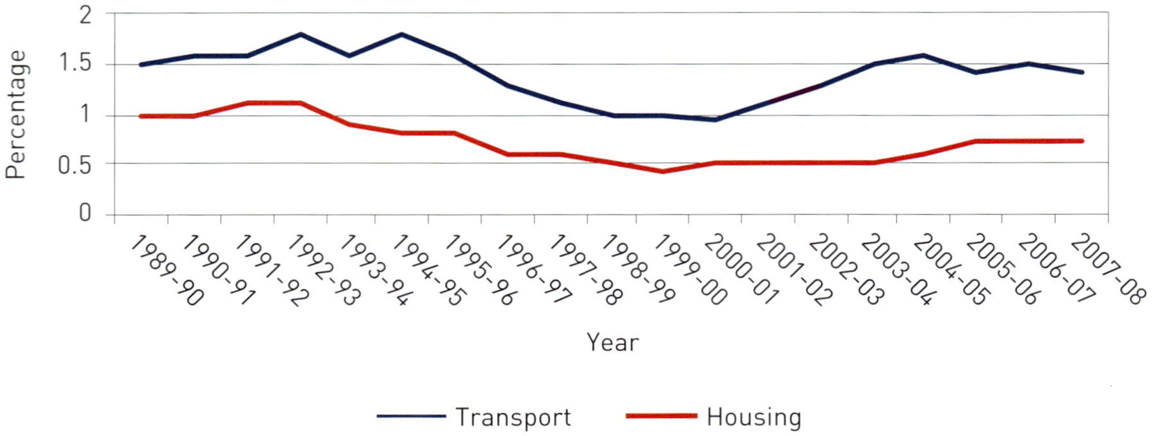

Source: Public Expenditure Statistical Analyses, HM Treasury, 2005

However, the Government may be counting too much on other sources. It is not clear that significant new affordable housing will be delivered through Section 106 agreements. Indeed, much of the affordable housing delivered through Section 106 also receives some public grant, particularly in London and the South East. While there may be the opportunity to use a land value tax in the future to capture value uplifts and help fund infrastructure improvements, this is a number of years away and there are requirements that need to be met in the short to medium term. However, the Government needs to give priority to the development of land value taxation.

There is no doubt that increasing the provision of affordable housing and transport infrastructure in the South East and other parts of the UK will require more public resources. It has been difficult to obtain detailed information from government departments on the expected infrastructure costs associated with the growth areas in the South East. The ODPM has commissioned some research on the local costs of delivering the infrastruture associated with increased housebuilding, although it is puzzling that this work was not undertaken as part of the development of the Sustainable Communities Plan before it was published. This has led to some criticism of the Government for its lack of transparency regarding the additional infrastructure costs. Part of the reason for this may, however, be because it can be difficult to provide a comprehensive assessment of the additional infrastructure needs associated with new developments. These infrastructure needs can range from providing additional roads and public transport services to extending the capacity of water and sewerage systems, ensuring adequate flood defences, and providing social and community infrastructure.

In terms of protection from flooding, the Government is already committed to a relatively generous settlement of £564 million per year on coastal and flood defences in England and Wales, over the period to 2007-08 (HMT, 2004). Developers are also expected to make a contribution to the cost of new flood defences where they are needed to protect new buildings. Of the new development planned for the South East growth areas, 30 per cent of the sites have been allocated in flood zone areas. The majority of these sites will be in areas where the annual probability of flooding is either low or moderate, mostly due to protection from existing flood defences (ABI, 2005). But the strategy of putting more development behind flood defences in these areas will raise the level of flood risk over the longer term. Across all the growth areas, flood management measures will need to be periodically reviewed to ensure a high standard of protection.

The case for water is different from other infrastructure considerations, as the costs of providing new water infrastructure will be largely borne by individual customers through their water bills. Water companies can also recover from the developer some of the costs of making new connections and upgrading the local networks. The Government is not expected to identify the funding necessary to meet additional water and sewerage infrastructure costs. Some additional water and sewerage costs associated with new housing developments in the South East were considered in the 2005-10 Water Price Review period (Ofwat, 2005). It is unclear, however, if that provided for is sufficient to maintain security of water supply and water quality. Water resources are already stretched in the South East and so one-off investments may be required in the short to medium term for large-scale assets such as reservoirs, which would increase water bills.

Additional transport infrastructure will need to be provided for from the public purse. In contrast to the Thames Gateway growth areas, the South East growth areas are dispersed throughout the region and the two largest growth areas are in the established urban centres of Milton Keynes and Ashford. The issue for these growth areas will be the additional costs of extending the capacity of existing transport infrastructure or improving existing transport services. Bids totalling £600 million were received by the CIF and these were whittled down to £225 million based on their deliverability (the funding can only be paid in 2006-07 and 2007-08) and the contribution they would make to housing growth. About 40 per cent of the bids being taken forward for appraisal under the CIF are in the South East growth areas (DfT, 2005b). However, it is worth putting the CIF into perspective – £200 million was little more than one per cent of the public sector spend on transport in 2004-05 (HMT, 2005). The CIF, as currently resourced, will be insufficient to meet the future additional transport infrastructure costs associated with the growth areas, particularly given the housing growth proposals in the Sustainable Communities Plan look out to 2016 and 2031.

Regardless of how many new homes are built in the South East in the coming years, it is already the case that the people of the South East have become more and more dependent on their cars. This is in part because the costs of motoring have been falling but also because there has been inadequate investment in public transport alternatives. The principal purpose of congestion charging is to reduce journey times and traffic jams in some of the busiest hot spots. However, congestion charging could also potentially raise extra resources to pay for future transport improvements. It is important to acknowledge that a national, comprehensive congestion charging scheme is unlikely to be something any government could implement any time soon.

If politicians are to win public support for national congestion charging, in the years preceding the introduction of the scheme there will need to be increased public spending on transport to offer accessible, reliable and cost-effective transport options. But this presents a funding conundrum – while a national congestion charging scheme could potentially raise additional revenue to pay for transport improvements it will not do so for at least another decade. Bearing in mind public spending on transport will be limited over the next parliamentary term, the Government is faced with the problem of how it can start to invest in transport improvements over the short to medium term to make the longer term introduction of a national congestion charging scheme publicly palatable.

There needs to be a national political consensus for giving greater priority to transport investment. One option is to increase transport investment by financing it through extra government borrowing. This would not have consequences for the Treasury's 'golden rule' which allows for borrowing to finance investment. It would, however, increase the debt-GDP ratio and therefore the future burden of interest payments to be borne by the taxpayer. These interest payments could be met by some of the future revenues raised from a national congestion charging scheme. This option could increase the pressure on any future government to introduce a national congestion charging scheme. However, without making a commitment to improve transport options and introduce national congestion charging over the longer term, we will simply be passing on the problems of rising congestion to future generations to solve.

A popular idea is that some of the future revenue raised from motorists should be redistributed back to the regions. But there is a trade-off between using the revenue gains from a national congestion charging scheme to fund upfront transport investment initially financed through borrowing, and using the revenue to pay for transport improvements in future decades. There will therefore need to be a balance between the two.

The 2004 Spending Review implied that after 2005-06, the overall rate of growth in public spending will decline significantly, with spending as a proportion of GDP reaching a plateau of about 42 per cent (HMT, 2004). Health, education and international development will remain priorities, with spending rising as a proportion of GDP, which of course implies that the share of some other areas of public spending will need to fall. The issues arising from the Commission's work suggests that policy-makers may have got some of their priorities wrong and that the relative neglect of housing and transport could undermine the delivery of the Government's Sustainable Communities Plan. It could also make it less likely that key policy challenges such as the introduction of a national congestion charging scheme will secure the necessary popular support. It may be time for a rethink of some of the Government's future priorities.

5. Improving governance and planning arrangements

There is a plethora of overlapping authorities and agencies in the South East, responsible for housing, planning and transport policy and delivery. The Commission's work has highlighted the need for better co-ordination both within the South East and across the Greater South East. There are a number of governance structures that could help to achieve this including the development of a single Housing, Planning and Transport Regional Board, the creation of a Greater South East Rail Authority and the establishment of a Greater South East Housing Forum. At the local level, local authorities are often best-placed to reflect and deliver on the priorities of the communities that they represent. Local authorities should be given greater responsibility for identifying appropriate housing needs and choosing the best ways to manage traffic demand in their area, within the context of an overarching regional framework. There is also a strong argument for greater integration of water resource and flood management into the development planning processes.

To help join up strategic policy-making at the regional level, the Government should create a single Housing, Planning and Transport Regional Board for advising ministers on strategic spending priorities across policy areas, as well as the possibility of switching funding between them. The Government has already proposed to integrate the existing Regional Housing Boards and Regional Planning Bodies (ODPM, 2004b) and the South East has been piloting an Experimental Regional Transport Board. The proposed Housing, Planning and Transport Board should support democratic accountability by being made up of elected local authority representatives from the Regional Assembly alongside senior representatives from business, the environmental and voluntary sectors, and relevant agencies. It should be led by a senior local politician. It should promote subsidiarity by not eroding the powers of local authorities. For example, the Board should account for the findings of Local Transport Plans when advising ministers on spending priorities on behalf of the region. Creating single Housing, Planning and Transport Regional Boards for the South East, East of England and London would help to streamline governance arrangements and make it easier to co-ordinate development and planning across the Greater South East.

To reflect the strong rail linkages between London, the South East and East of England, the Government should create a Greater South East Rail Authority with responsibility for the franchising of rail passenger services across the Greater South East (excluding inter-city rail journeys). The 2004 Future of Rail White Paper recognised that central government is not always best placed to take decisions on the transport needs of different communities and that in future, the devolved administrations would take increased responsibilities for rail passenger services (DfT, 2004b). The 2005 Railways Act that followed, gave Transport for London (TfL) the ability to enter into a franchise agreement with the approval of the Secretary of State (House of Lords, 2005). The Act requires TfL to add two extra board members from the South East and East of England. Nonetheless, the TfL board will still be dominated by people representing London's interests. Moreover, with the exception of the Mayor of London, the board of TfL is not elected.

A more pluralistic proposal would be to devolve responsibility for the franchising of rail passenger services to a new Greater South East Rail Authority. A pragmatic step would be to make TfL the executive body responsible for implementing the decisions of the authority. This would have the advantage of enabling the integration of local and regional rail services with the other road and public transport services which TfL already has responsibility for in Greater London. This would allow integration of fares, timetables, ticketing and passenger information across transport services. This broader remit might justify a name change for TfL. However, of far greater importance is the need to ensure democratic accountability, with the new rail authority governed by a board of politically elected representatives drawn from London, the South East and East of England. The new rail authority would need to work closely with both TfL and Network Rail, which is responsible for operating and maintaining the rail network.

There is also a need for strategic oversight in relation to housing across the Greater South East. One way of doing this would be to establish a Greater South East Housing Forum where the regional authorities in London, the South East and East of England could meet. Many housing experts have argued that the Greater South East functions as effectively one integrated housing market (e.g. Bramley, 2005) with a close inter-relationship between the three regions in terms of population movements (see chapter 3). Yet there is currently no mechanism for these regions to adequately reflect inter-regional issues in their strategies. This forum should not have any powers of intervention in regional strategies. Rather, it would be up to each region to respond accordingly to the inter-regional issues presented. Importantly, however, this would be done in a open and transparent way.

In addition, there is a need for a more flexible approach to housing planning periods. The South East Plan is due to set the policy framework for housing between 2006 and 2026. But given the limitations in housing data, including uncertainty over future international migration patterns, setting housebuilding targets for 20 years hence does not seem sensible. Shorter planning horizons may be more appropriate, enabling more flexible and strategic responses to housing needs in the South East.

Across the South East, there needs to be a locally sensitive approach to planning and delivering new development, which requires strong leadership by local authorities. As elected bodies, local authorities have a legitimacy that can allow them to deal with contentious issues in a way that enables greater public understanding and acceptance of those issues. This could include handling potentially difficult issues relating to environmentally sensitive land or housing densities. It should be up to local authorities to identify the appropriate balance of affordable housing needs (i.e. the mix of socially rented and intermediate housing) within their communities. They should be responsive to changing needs over time and promote the development of mixed communities.

Local authorities often complain that one of the biggest blocks to bringing forward new development is the lack of incentives. The funding of local infrastructure improvements alongside new developments is often seen a critical issue by residents (ICM, 2005). If new developments, particularly affordable housing, were prioritised for local infrastructure funding, this could provide local authorities with the incentive they need to win public support for new developments.

For water resources and flood management, there is a strong case for involving water companies more directly in the planning process as statutory consultees, and for development plans to be undertaken in tandem with water resource and flood management plans. Local Development Frameworks (LDFs) and Regional Spatial Strategies (RSSs) need to better integrate issues relating to the availability of water resources and the impact on water quality over the lifetime of the development, as well as incorporate strategic flood assessments. These measures will help to ensure that the cost and limits of water and sewerage infrastructure requirements are fully understood. It would also help identify the areas where water scarcity, water quality and/or flood risk issues are so severe that they may be grounds for refusal of planning permission.

There also needs to be greater clarity over the co-ordination of, and responsibility for, sewerage and drainage issues, especially as the incidence of urban flooding is likely to increase over the following decades. The best way to mitigate flood risk is to direct new developments away from high risk flood zone areas. Local Planning Authorities (LPAs) and developers should give more consideration to the insurance implications of building in flood zones and behind existing flood defences. It is welcome that the Government is consulting on how the Environment Agency could be made a statutory consultee for all new developments in flood risk locations (Defra, 2005b). As a last resort, the Government may have to intervene to ensure that no inappropriate development takes place in flood zone areas.

Conclusions

If the South East is to maintain its economic success, while enhancing the environment and improving the wellbeing and quality of life of all its citizens, it will need to develop a new approach to growth and consumption. The focus for policy should be on achieving a sustainable rate of growth in output per head and disposable household income, rather than just maximising the growth in GDP. Policy-makers in the South East and in government need to develop measures that influence the behaviour of individuals and firms, to enable and encourage the more efficient use of natural resources that results in less pollution and waste. There will need to be investments in infrastructure, particularly public transport improvements for helping to reduce car dependency.

If the South East is to improve the wellbeing of all its citizens, reducing economic disparities within the region and improving the availability of affordable housing will be essential. The key to reducing disparities will be to raise employment rates in less prosperous parts of the South East and for disadvantaged groups. There will need to be additional public funding for meeting affordable housing needs.

From the point of view of the South East, boosting the economic performance of the less prosperous regions in the UK would make it easier for the region to cope with the problems that current levels of relative economic prosperity pose. This would help to ease the pressures on the region that have been generated by the relative shift in economic activity and population to the Greater South East. The Government should particularly focus on enhancing policies in relation to employment services and skills, to raise employment rates in less prosperous regions.

An approach to growth driven by quality of life priorities that seeks to promote resource efficiency, reduce disparities within the region and support government efforts to address inter-regional disparities in economic performance, would be in the long term interest of the South East.

Abbreviations

ABI	Association of British Insurers
EU	European Union
CIF	Community Infrastructure Fund
Defra	Department for Environment, Food and Rural Affairs
DfES	Department for Education and Skills
DfT	Department for Transport
DTI	Department of Trade and Industry
DWP	Department for Work and Pensions
EEC	Energy Efficiency Commitment
ELL	Economic Level of Leakage
GDP	Gross Domestic Product
GLA	Greater London Authority
GOSE	Government Office for the South East
GVA	Gross Value Added
HMT	HM Treasury
HoC	House of Commons
IMD	Index of Multiple Deprivation
LCHO	Low Cost Home Ownership
LDFs	Local Development Frameworks
LPAs	Local Planning Authorities
NTS	National Travel Survey
NUTS	Nomenclature of Units for Territorial Statistics
OECD	Organisation for Economic Co-operation and Development
ODPM	Office of the Deputy Prime Minister
Ofwat	Office of Water Services
ONS	Office for National Statistics
pcc	per capita consumption
PPG	Planning Policy Guidance
PPS	Planning Policy Statement
PSA	Public Service Agreement
PWS	Public Water Supply
RSSs	Regional Spatial Strategies
RSL	Registered Social Landlords
SEEDA	South East England Development Agency
SEERA	South East England Regional Assembly
STW	Sewage Treatment Works
SuDs	Sustainable Urban Drainage Systems
SWERDA	South West of England Regional Development Agency
TfL	Transport for London
TIF	Transport Innovation Fund
VED	Vehicle Excise Duty
WCED	World Commission on Environment and Development
WRSE Group	Water Resources in the South East Group

References

References for chapter 1 – The problems of success: quality of life priorities in the South East

ABI (2004) *Strategic Planning for Flood Risk in the Growth Areas – Insurance Considerations.* Association of British Insurers.

Defra (2005) *UK Sustainable Development Strategy.* Department for Environment, Food and Rural Affairs.

Defra (2002) *Survey of Public Attitudes to Quality of Life and to the Environment.* Department for Environment, Food and Rural Affairs.

Easterlin R (1974) 'Does Economic Growth Improve the Human Lot?' in David P and Reder M (eds) *Nations and Households in Economic Growth: Essays in Honour of Moses Abramovitz.* New York Press Association.

Environment Agency (2004) *State of the Environment 2004.* South East England Environment Agency.

Foley J (2004) *The Problems of Success. Reconciling Economic Growth and Quality of Life in the South East.* Working Paper One, Commission on Sustainable Development in the South East. ippr.

Levett R, Christie I, Jacobs M and Therivel R (2003) *A Better Choice of Choice. Quality of Life, Consumption and Economic Growth.* Fabian Society.

MORI (2004) *The South East Plan – Wave 1 and Wave 2. Evaluation of Residents' Attitudes Towards the Region.* Research Study conducted for the South East England Regional Assembly.

NTS (2003) *National Travel Survey.* Data on travel patterns across Great Britain.

ODPM (2003) *Sustainable Communities: Building for the Future.* Office of the Deputy Prime Minister.

UKCIP (2002) *Climate Change Scenarios.* UK Climate Impacts Programme.

WCED (1987) *Our Common Future.* The Brundtland Report for the World Commission on Environment and Development.

References for chapter 2 – A successful region: the South East's economic performance

Adams J, Robinson P, and Vigor A (2003) *A New Regional Policy for the UK.* ippr.

Brooks R (2004) *Pay and the Public Service Workforce.* ippr.

DfES (2003) *The Skills for Life Survey.* Department for Education and Skills, Research Brief RB490.

DWP (2005) *Five Year Strategy: Opportunity and Security Throughout Life.* Department for Work and Pensions.

DWP/ONS (2005) *Client Group Analysis: Quarterly Bulletin on the Population of Working Age on Key Benefits – November 2004*. Department for Work and Pensions/Office for National Statistics, March 2005.

EC (2005) *Working Together for Growth and Jobs: A New Start for the Lisbon Strategy*. European Commission. Communication from Barroso in agreement with the Vice-President Verheugen to the Spring European Council, February 2005.

Eurostat/EC (2004) *Third Report on Economic and Social Cohesion: Main Regional Indicators*. Eurostat/ European Commission, Brussels.

EBS (2004) *Trend Growth Rates in the UK Regions*. Experian Business Strategies.

GLA Economics (2004), 'A Focus on Cities' in *London's Economy Today*, April 2004.

HMT (2004) *Spending Review 2004*. HM Treasury.

Huggins R (2001) *Global Index of Regional Knowledge Economies: Benchmarking South East England*. Final report prepared for SEEDA, November 2001, Robert Huggins Associates.

Huggins R (2003) *Global Index of Regional Knowledge Economies 2003 Update: Benchmarking South East England*. Final report prepared to SEEDA, October 2003, Robert Huggins Associates.

Kent County Council (2005) *The Kent Local Area Agreement, April 2005 – March 2008*. Kent County Council.

LSC (2003) *National Employers Skills Survey*. Learning and Skills Council.

LSE/Corporation of London (2003) *London's place in the UK Economy 2003*. London School of Economics and Corporation of London.

OECD (2003) *OECD Science, Technology and Industry Scoreboard*. Organisation for Economic Co-operation and Development.

OECD (2004) *Economic Surveys: United Kingdom, 2004*. Organisation for Economic Co-operation and Development.

ODPM (2005) *Sustainable Communities: People, Places and Prosperity*. A five-year plan from the Office of the Deputy Prime Minister.

ODPM/ONS (2005) *Key Statistics for Urban Areas in England and Wales*. Office of the Deputy Prime Minister/Office for National Statistics, June 2004.

ONS (2005) *Regional Household Income*. First Release. Office for National Statistics, April 2005.

ONS (2004a) *Regional Gross Value Added*. First Release. Office for National Statistics, December 2004.

ONS (2004b) *Local Gross Value Added*. First Release. Office for National Statistics, December 2004.

ONS (2004c) *Employment Rate by Travel to Work Area, 2002*. Map supplied to ippr from the Office for National Statistics.

ONS/LFS (2004) *Regional Trends 38, 2004 Edition*. Office for National Statistics, Tables 14.8, 15.7, 16.6, 17.5 and Annual Local Area Labour Force Survey 2002-03.

Oxford Economic Forecasting (2004) *London's Linkages with the Rest of the UK*. OEF/Corporation of London.

SEEDA (2002) *The Regional Economic Strategy for South East England*. South East England Development Agency.

SEEDA (2005a) *Draft SEEDA Corporate Plan 2005-2008*. South East England Development Agency.

SEEDA (2005b) 'South East Plan', in *South East View*, Spring 2005. South East England Development Agency.

SEEDA (2005c) *Sustaining Success in a Prosperous Region: Economic Implications of the South East Plan*. South East England Development Agency/Deloitte, March 2005.

SEERA (2005) *South East Plan: Consultation Draft*. South East England Regional Assembly, January 2005.

University of Warwick (2003-04) *Working Futures Regional Report, 2003-04*. Institute for Employment Research, University of Warwick.

References for chapter 3 – Meeting housing need in the South East

Barker K (2004) *Barker Review of Housing Supply: securing our future housing needs*. Final Report. HM Treasury and Office of the Deputy Prime Minister.

Barker K (2003) *Barker Review of Housing Supply: securing our future housing needs*. Interim Report. HM Treasury and Office of the Deputy Prime Minister.

Bramley G (2005) *Research Analysis on Demand, Supply and Affordability*. Paper prepared for the ippr Commission on Sustainable Development in the South East. Copies available from ippr on request.

Bramley G (1998) 'Housing Surpluses and Housing Need' in Lowe S, Spencer S and Keenan P (eds.) *Housing Abandonment in Britain: studies in the causes and effects of low demand housing*. Centre for Housing Policy Conference Papers, University of York.

Bramley G (1996) *Housing with Hindsight*. Campaign for the Protection of Rural England.

Bramley G and Karley N. K (forthcoming) 'Affordability, Need and the Intermediate Market: Measurement, Change and Significance.' Submitted to *Housing Studies*.

Bramley G and Smart G (1995) *Rural Incomes and Housing Affordability*. Rural Development Commission.

Crook T, Currie J, Jackson A, Monk S, Rowley S, Smith K and Whitehead C (2002) *Planning Gain and Affordable Housing: making it count*. Joseph Rowntree Foundation.

DETR (1999) *Projections of Households in England to 2021*. Department of the Environment, Transport and the Regions.

Egan J (2004) *The Egan Review: skills for sustainable communities*. Office of the Deputy Prime Minister.

Gardiner J (2005) 'ODPM Offer Help to Broaden Right to Buy' in *Regeneration and Renewal*, 28 January, 3.

GLA (2004) *The London Plan*. Greater London Authority.

HMT (2005) *Public Expenditure Statistical Analyses*. HM Treasury.

Holmans A (2004) *Housing Need in the South East*. South East England Regional Assembly.

Holmans A, Monk S, and Whitehead C (2004) *Building for the Future – 2004 Update: a report of the Shelter Housing Investment Project*. Shelter.

Housing Corporation (2004) *New Partnerships in Affordable Housing: a pilot investment programme open to Housing Associations and unregistered bodies*. Housing Corporation.

Housing Corporation (2003) *A Home of My Own. Supporting paper for Home Ownership Task Force*. Housing Corporation.

Huhne C (2004) *Why We Should Follow Pittsburgh*. New Statesman, 27 October, 38-39.

ICM (2005) *South East Plan Research Results: prepared for the South East Counties*. ICM.

IMD (2004). *Index of Multiple Deprivation*. Online data source from the Office of the Deputy Prime Minister: www.odpm.gov.uk.

Imrie R and Raco M (eds) (2003) *Urban Renaissance? New Labour, community and urban policy.* Policy Press.

Monk S, Crook T, Lister D, Rowley S, Short C and Whitehead C (2005). *Land and Finance for Affordable Housing: the complementary roles of Social Housing Grant and the provision of affordable housing through the planning system.* Joseph Rowntree Foundation.

ODPM (2005a) *Homes for All.* Office of the Deputy Prime Minister.

ODPM (2005b) *Housebuilding: permanent dwellings completed by tenure.* On line data source from the Office of the Deputy Prime Minister: www.odpm.gov.uk.

ODPM (2005c) *Housebuilding: January to March quarter 2005.* ODPM News Release, 12 May 2005. Office of the Deputy Prime Minister.

ODPM (2005d) *Key Regional Housing Priorities Receive Multi-Billion Pound Boost,* ODPM News Release, 22 March 2005. Office of the Deputy Prime Minister.

ODPM (2004a) *Household Estimates and Projections: interim 2002 household projections: by region, 2001-2021.* Online data source from the Office of the Deputy Prime Minister: www.odpm.gov.uk.

ODPM (2004b) *Permanent Dwellings Completed by Tenure and Region.* Online data source from the Office of the Deputy Prime Minister: www.odpm.gov.uk.

ODPM (2004c) *Housing and Planning in the Regions: consultation.* Office of the Deputy Prime Minister.

ODPM (2004d) *Three-year Revenue and Capital Settlements: consultation paper.* Office of the Deputy Prime Minister.

ODPM (2003) *Sustainable Communities: building for the future.* Office of the Deputy Prime Minister.

Piatt S, Fawcett W and De Carteret R (2004) *Housing Futures: informed public opinion.* Joseph Rowntree Foundation.

Planning Resource (2005) *New Development Tax for Milton Keynes Growth.* Planning Resource – 14 April 2005. On line data source from Planning Resource: www.planning.haynet.com.

Prime Minister's Strategy Unit and Office of the Deputy Prime Minister (2005) *Improving the Prospects of People Living in Areas of Multiple Deprivation in England.* Cabinet Office.

SEERA (2005) *The South East Plan: Consultation Draft.* South East England Regional Assembly.

SEERA (2004) *Regional Monitoring Report 2004.* South East England Regional Assembly.

SWERDA (2005) *The Way Ahead: delivering sustainable communities in the South West.* South West of England Regional Development Agency.

Wilcox S (2004) *UK Housing Review 2004/2005.* Chartered Institute of Housing and the Council of Mortgage Lenders.

Wilcox S (2003) *Can Work, Can't Buy.* Joseph Rowntree Foundation.

References for chapter 4 – Transport: keeping the South East moving

Barker K (2004) *Review of Housing Supply. Delivering Stability: Securing Future Housing Needs.* Report commissioned by HM Treasury and the Office of the Deputy Prime Minister.

Brighton and Hove City Council (2005) Information about the 'Breeze up to the Downs' initiative from the Brighton and Hove City Council Web-site: www.brighton-hove.gov.uk.

Brighton and Hove City Council (2003) *Bus Information Strategy.*

Brighton and Hove City Council (2000) *Local Transport Plan.*

Buckinghamshire County Council (2003) *Annual Progress Report 2002/03.*

CBI (2004) *Is Transport Holding the UK Back?* Confederation of British Industry.

CfIT (2001) *European Best Practice in Delivering Integrated Transport. Key Findings.* WS Atkins report for the Commission for Integrated Transport.

EC (2004) *European Economy.* European Commission, Directorate General for Economic and Financial Affairs.

European Foundation (2000) *Third European Survey of Working Conditions.* European Foundation for the Improvement of Living and Working Conditions.

Defra (2005) *Provisional 2004 UK Climate Change Sustainable Development Indicator and 2003 Air Pollutant Emissions Final Figures.* Statistical Release, 31 March 2005. Department for Environment, Food and Rural Affairs.

DETR (1999) *Transport and the Economy, Report of the Standing Advisory Committee on Trunk Road Assessment.* Department of Tranport, Environment and the Regions.

DfT (2005a) *The Future of Transport: Modelling and Analysis.* Department for Transport

DfT (2005b) *New Transport Schemes to Support Housing Development in the Wider South East.* DfT News Release, 17 March 2005. Department for Transport.

DfT (2005c) *Carpool Lane on the Cards for the M25.* DfT News Release, 20 March 2005. Department for Transport.

DfT (2004a) *Transport Statistics Bulletin: Road Goods Travelling to Mainland Europe.* Department for Transport.

DfT (2004b) *Regional Transport Statistics.* Department for Transport.

DfT (2004c) *The Future of Transport. A Network for 2030.* Department for Transport.

DfT (2004d) *Road Pricing Feasibility Study. Initial Assessment of Regional Impacts.* Note provided by the Department for Transport to ippr in December 2004.

DfT (2004e) *A Bulletin of Public Transport Statistics.* Great Britain, 2004 Edition. Department for Transport.

DfT (2004f) *Darling Announces First Congestion Busting Motorway Lane.* DfT News Release, 9 December 2004. Department for Transport.

DfT (2004g) *Smarter Choices – Changing the Way We Travel.* Report published by the Department for Transport by Robert Gordon University in Aberdeen, Eco-Logica, Transport for Quality of Life and the ESRC Transport Studies Unit at University College London.

DfT (2004h) *The Future of Rail.* Department for Transport.

DfT (2003) *Transport Statistics Bulletin: Transport of Goods by Road in Britain.* Department for Transport.

DfT (2001) *Powering Future Vehicles Strategy.* Department for Transport.

Ekins P and Dresner S (2004) *Green Taxes and Charges*. Joseph Rowntree Foundation.

Foley J (2004) *The Problems of Success: Reconciling Economic Growth and Quality of Life in the South East*. Working Paper Two, Commission on Sustainable Development in the South East. ippr.

Foley J (2003) *Tomorrow's Low Carbon Cars. Driving Innovation and Long Term Investment in Low Carbon Cars*. ippr.

Glaister S and Graham D (2003) *Transport Pricing and Investment in England*. Research commissioned by the Independent Transport Commission.

GOSE (2004) *Regional Transport Strategy for the South East*. Government Office for the South East.

GOSE (2002) *Multi-Modal Study for the South East Coast Corridor*. Report by Halcrow Group Ltd prepared for the Government Office for the South East.

GOSE (2000) *Access to Hastings Multi-Modal Study*. Government Office for the South East.

Grayling T, Sansom N and Foley J (2004) *In the Fast Lane*. ippr.

Grayling T, Hallam K, Graham D, Anderson R and Glaister S (2002) *Streets Ahead – Safe and Liveable Streets for Children*. ippr.

Hall P (2004) *Is the Greater South East a Mega-City Region?* An essay commissioned by ippr on behalf of the Commission on Sustainable Development in the South East.

Hamilton-Baillie B (2001) *Home Zones: Reconciling People, Places and Transport*. Harvard University.

Headicar P (2003) 'Land Use Planning and the Management of Transport Demand' in Hine J and Preston J and Ashgate (eds.) *Integrated Futures and Transport Choices*.

Headicar P (2000) 'The Exploding City Region: Should it, Can it be Reversed?' in Williams K, Jenks M and Burton E (eds.) *Achieving Sustainable Urban Form*.

HMSO (1963) *Traffic in Towns: A Study of the Long Term Problem of Traffic in Towns*. Report of the Steering Group and Working Group appointed by the Minister of Transport, known as the Buchanan report. Her Majesty's Stationery Office.

HMT (2005a) *Public Expenditure Statistical Analyses 2005*. HM Treasury.

HMT (2005b) *Budget 2005 – Investing for Our Future: Fairness and Opportunity for Britain's Hard Working Families*. HM Treasury.

HMT/HM C&E/DfT (2005) *Modernising the Taxation of the Haulage Industry: Lorry Road User Charge*. HM Treasury, HM Customs and Excise, Department for Transport.

HMT (2004a) *Spending Review 2004*. HM Treasury.

HMT (2004b) *Modernising the Taxation of the Road Haulage Industry – Lorry Road User Charge. Progress Report Three*. HM Treasury.

HMT (2003) *Modernising the Taxation of the Road Haulage Industry – Lorry Road User Charge. Progress Report Two*. HM Treasury.

HMT/DfT/ODPM/DTI (2004) *Devolving Decision Making: A Consultation on Regional Funding Allocations*. HM Treasury, Department for Transport, Office of the Deputy Prime Minister and Department of Trade and Industry.

HoC Transport Select Committee (2005) *Road Pricing: The Next Steps*. Seventh Report of Session 2004-05. House of Commons Transport Select Committee.

House of Lords (2005) *The Railways Bill*. HL Bill 51 – 53/4. Published by authority of the House of Lords, London. The Stationery Office Ltd.

NTS (1985-86 to 2003) *National Travel Survey*. Data on travel patterns across Great Britain made available to ippr.

MORI (2004) *The South East Plan – Wave 1 and 2*. Evaluation of Residents' Attitudes Towards the Region. Research Study Conducted for the South East England Regional Assembly.

ODPM (2004) *Housing and Planning in the Regions*. Consultation. Office of the Deputy Prime Minister.

ODPM (2003) *Sustainable Communities: Building for the Future*. Office of the Deputy Prime Minister.

ONS (2004) 'The Impact of UK Households on the Environment in 2001'. *Economic Trends*, 611. Office for National Statistics, October 2004.

Parliamentary Answer, Tony McNulty (2004) The Parliamentary Under-Secretary of State for Transport, 166176, 20 April 2004: Column 148. House of Commons.

Power A (2004) *Definition and Components of Sustainable Communities*. London School of Economics. Paper to a seminar held by the Sustainable Development Commission, 5 October 2004.

RAC Foundation (2002) *Motoring Towards 2050*. RAC Foundation.

SEEDA (2002) *The Regional Economic Strategy for South East England*. South East England Development Agency.

SEERA (2005) *South East Plan: Consultation Draft*. South East England Regional Assembly.

SUSTRANS (2004) *TravelSmart 2004 Update*. SUSTRANS.

SUSTRANS (2002) *TravelSmart Frome Pilot Project*. SUSTRANS.

TfL (2005) *London's Railways. The Case for a London Regional Rail Authority*. Transport for London.

TfL (2004) *Central London Congestion Charging: Impacts Monitoring Second Annual Report*. Transport for London.

References for chapter 5 – Troubled waters: water resources and flooding in the South East

ABI (2004) *Strategic Planning for Flood Risk in the Growth Areas – Insurance Considerations*. Association of British Insurers.

ABI (2005) *Making Communities Sustainable*. Association of British Insurers.

Brown J D and Damery S L (2002) 'Managing Flood Risk in the UK: Towards an Integration of Social and Technical Perspectives' in *Transactions of the Institute of British Geographers* 27, 412-426.

Defra (2005a) *Securing the Future. Delivering the UK sustainable development strategy*. Department for Environment, Food and Rural Affairs.

Defra (2005b) *Making Space for Water. Developing a new Government strategy for Flood and Coastal Erosion Risk Management in England*. First Government reponse to the autumn 2004 Making space for water consultation exercise, March 2005. Department for Environment, Food and Rural Affairs.

Defra (2004a) *Energy Efficiency: The Government's Plan for Action*. Department for Environment, Food and Rural Affairs.

Defra (2004b) *Making Space for Water. Developing a new Government strategy for Flood and Coastal Erosion Risk Management in England.* A consultation exercise, July 2004. Department for Environment, Food and Rural Affairs.

Defra (2004c) *Strategy for Flood and Coastal Erosion Risk Management: Groundwater Flooding Scoping Study* (LDS 23). Department for Environment, Food and Rural Affairs.

DETR and Welsh Office (1999) *Taking Water Responsibly. Government Decisions Following Consultation on Changes to the Water Abstraction Licensing System in England and Wales.* Department of the Environment, Transport and the Regions.

DTI and DEFRA (2004) *Energy White Paper.* Department of Trade and Industry and Department for Environment, Food and Rural Affairs.

DTI and DEFRA (2001) *The UK Fuel Poverty Strategy.* Department of Trade and Industry and Department for Environment, Food and Rural Affairs.

Edwards K and Martin L (1995) 'A Methodology for Surveying Domestic Water Consumption' in *The Chartered Institute of Water and Environmental Management*, 9, 477-488.

Ekins P and Dresner S (2004) *Green Taxes and Charges.* Joseph Rowntree Foundation.

Enarson E and Fordham M (2001) 'Lines that divide, ties that bind: race, class and gender in women's flood recovery in the US and UK' in *Australian Journal of Emergency Management* 15 (4): 43-52.

ENDS Report (2004) 'Water leakage figures: fact or fiction?' in *ENDS Report* No. 358, November 2004.

Environment Agency (2005a) *Water Situation Report.* Monthly bulletin for England and Wales March 2005. Environment Agency.

Environment Agency (2005b) *High Level Target 12, Development and Flood Risk 2003/04.* Joint report to Department for Environment, Food and Rural Affairs and the Office of the Deputy Prime Minister by the Environment Agency and Local Government Association.

Environment Agency (2004a) *State of the Environment.* Environment Agency 2004.

Environment Agency (2004b) *Maintaining Water Supply.* The Environment Agency's advice to Ministers on the final water resources plans submitted by water companies as part of the 2004 periodic review, July 2004. Environment Agency.

Environment Agency (2001) *Water Resources for the Future. A Strategy for the Southern Region.* Environment Agency.

Fitch M and Price H (2002) *Water Poverty in England and Wales.* Public Utilities Access Forum.

Foresight (2004) *Future Flooding.* Office of Science and Technology, Department of Trade and Industry.

Herrington P R (1998) 'Analyising and Forecasting Peak Demands on the Public Water Supply' in *Journal of the Chartered Institute of Water and Environmental Management*, 12, 139-143.

HoC (1998) *Water Industry Bill 1998-99.* House of Commons Library, Research Paper 98/117. House of Commons.

HoC Environment, Food and Rural Affairs Select Committee (2004) *Climate Change, Water Security and Flooding.* Sixteenth report of 2003-04 session, Evidence 9, Question 19. House of Commons Environment, Food and Rural Affairs Select Committee.

HoC Environment, Food and Rural Affairs Select Committee (2003) *Water Pricing.* First Report of Session 2003-04. House of Commons Environment, Food and Rural Affairs Select Committee.

HMT (2004) *2004 Spending Review*. HM Treasury.

MORI (2004) *The South East Plan – Wave 1 and 2*. Evaluation of Residents' Attitudes Towards the Region. Research Study Conducted for the South East England Regional Assembly.

Mulholland Research and Consulting (2004) *Attitudes and Decision Making Among Home Buyers*. Prepared for Commission for Architecture and the Built Environment, World Wildlife Fund and Halifax Bank of Scotland.

NCC (2002) *Towards a Sustainable Water Charging Policy*. National Consumer Council.

ODPM (2005) *Sustainable Communities: Homes for All*. Five Year Plan from the Office of the Deputy Prime Minister.

ODPM (2004) *Statistical Release. Land Use Change in England to 2003: additional tables. LUCS-19A* The Office of the Deputy Prime Minister.

ODPM (2003) *Sustainable Communities: Building for the Future*. Office of the Deputy Prime Minister.

ODPM (2001) *Planning Policy Guidance Note 25: Development and Flood Risk*. Office of the Deputy Prime Minister.

Ofwat (2005a) *Letter to ippr from the Office of Water Services*. 9 May, 2005.

Ofwat (2005b) *Information on Water Metering, Water Efficiency and Water Infrastructure Costs*. On line data source from the Office of Water Services: www.ofwat.org.

Ofwat (2004a) *Security of Supply, Leakage and the Efficient Use of Water*. 2003 – 2004 report. Office of Water Services.

Ofwat (2004b) *Water Price Review*. Office of Water Services.

Rydin Y (2004) *Planning, Sustainability and Environmental Risks*. Office of the Deputy Prime Minister.

SEERA (2005) *South East Plan: Consultation Draft*. South East England Regional Assembly.

Sustainable Buildings Task Group (2004) *Better Buildings – Better Lives*. Sustainable Buildings Task Group Report. Report to the Office of the Deputy Prime Minister, Department of the Environment, Food and Rural Affairs and Department of Trade and Industry.

Thames Water Utilities (2004) *Strategic Business Plan for the 2004 Periodic Review*. Thames Water Utilities.

UKCIP (2002) *Climate Change scenarios*. UK Climate Impacts Programme.

Walker G J et al. (2003) *Environmental Quality and Social Deprivation*. Environment Agency.

WRSE Group (2005) *Examination of Water Supply-Demand Balance Impacts of Housing Growth Scenarios of the Draft South East Plan*. Water Resources in the South East Group.

WRSE Group (2004) *A Contribution to Preparation of the South East Plan, from the Water Resources in the South East Group*. Water Resources in the South East Group.

References for chapter 6 – The Commission's key findings: cross cutting themes

ABI (2005) *Making Communities Sustainable*. Association of British Insurers.

Barker K (2004) *Barker Review of Housing Supply: Securing Our Future Housing Needs*. Final report. HM Treasury and the Office of the Deputy Prime Minister.

Bramley G (2005) *Research Analysis on Housing Demand, Supply and Affordability*. Paper prepared for ippr's Commission on Sustainable Development in the South East.

Defra (2005a) *Delivering the Essentials of Life*. Defra's 5 Year Strategy. Department for Environment, Food and Rural Affairs.

Defra (2005b) *Making Space for Water. Developing a new Government strategy for Flood and Coastal Erosion Risk Management in England*. First Government reponse to the Autumn 2004 'Making Space for Water' consultation exercise. March 2005. Department for Environment, Food and Rural Affairs

DfT (2005a) *The Future of Transport: Modelling and Analysis*. Department for Transport.

DfT (2005b) *New Transport Schemes to Support Housing Development in the Wider South East*. DfT News Release, 17th March 2005. Department for Transport.

DfT (2004a) *Smarter Choices – Changing the Way We Travel*. Report published by the Department for Transport by Robert Gordon University in Aberdeen, Eco-Logica, Transport for Quality of Life and the ESRC Transport Studies Unit at University College London.

DfT (2004b) *The Future of Rail*. Department for Transport.

DWP (2005) *Five Year Strategy: Opportunity and Security Throughout Life*. Department for Work and Pensions.

EBS (2004) *Trend Growth Rates in the UK Regions*. Experian Business Strategies.

Environment Agency (2004) *State of the Environment in the South East*. Environment Agency.

Environment Agency (2001) *Water Resources for the Future. A Strategy for the Southern Region*. Environment Agency.

Ekins P and Dresner S (2004) *Green Taxes and Charges*. Joseph Rowntree Foundation.

Fitch M and Price H (2002) *Water Poverty in England and Wales*. Public Utilities Access Forum.

Foresight (2004) *Future Flooding*. Office of Science and Technology, Department of Trade and Industry.

GOSE (2002) *Multi-Modal Study for the South East Coast Corridor*. Report by Halcrow Group Ltd prepared for the Government Office for the South East.

HMT (2005) *Public Expenditure Statistical Analyses 2005*. HM Treasury.

HMT (2004) *Spending Review 2004*. HM Treasury.

House of Lords (2005) *The Railways Bill*. HL Bill 51 – 53/4. Published by authority of the House of Lords, London. The Stationery Office Ltd.

ICM (2005) *South East Plan Research Results: prepared for the South East Counties*. ICM.

LSC (2003) *National Employers Skills Survey*. Learning and Skills Council.

LSE/Corporation of London (2003) *London's Place in the UK Economy 2003*. London School of Economics/Corporation of London.

MORI (2004) *The South East Plan – Wave 1 and 2. Evaluation of Residents' Attitudes Towards the Region*. Research Study Conducted for the South East England Regional Assembly.

NTS (1985-86 to 2003) *National Travel Survey*. Data on travel patterns across Great Britain made available to ippr.

ODPM (2005) *Housebuilding: January to March Quarter 2005*. ODPM News Release, 12th May 2005. Office of the Deputy Prime Minister.

ODPM (2004a) *Household Estimates and Projections: Interim 2002 Household Projections: By Region 2001-2021*. Data available online: www.odpm.gov.uk.

ODPM (2004b) *Housing and Planning in the Regions*. Consultation. Office of the Deputy Prime Minister.

ODPM (2003) *Sustainable Communities: Building for the Future*. Office of the Deputy Prime Minister.

Ofwat (2005) *Information on Water Metering, Water Efficiency and Water Infrastructure Costs*. On line data source from the Office of Water Services: www.ofwat.org.

ONS (2004) 'The Impact of UK Households on the Environment in 2001'. *Economic Trends*, 611. Office for National Statistics, October 2004.

ONS (2003) *Mid Year Population Estimates for 2002-03*. Office for National Statistics.

SEEDA (2005) *Sustaining Success in a Prosperous Region: Economic Implications of the South East Plan*. South East England Development Agency/ Deloitte.

SEEDA (2002) *The Regional Economic Strategy for South East England*. South East England Development Agency.

SEERA (2005) *South East Plan: Consultation Draft*. South East England Regional Assembly.

UK Climate Impacts Programme (2002) *Climate Change Scenarios*. UK Climate Impacts Programme.

WRSE Group (2005) *Examination of Water Supply-Demand Balance Impacts of Housing Growth Scenarios of the Draft South East Plan*. Water Resources in the South East Group.

WRSE Group (2004) *A Contribution to Preparation of the South East Plan*. Water Resources in the South East Group.

Appendices

Appendix for chapter 3 – Meeting housing need in the South East

Levels of housebuilding

This appendix will present the levels of housebuilding that have been recommended by government, the SEERA officials and SEERA members and Bramley (2005). It is often not entirely clear where the precise headline figures that are quoted come from, which makes interpretation difficult.

Regional Planning Guidance and the Sustainable Communities Plan

The current government housebuilding target for the South East is 29,500, applicable until 2006. This figure represents the South East's Regional Planning Guidance (RPG9) and the commitments under the Sustainable Communities Plan. After 2006 the Regional Spatial Strategy – the South East Plan – will set the target.

Original Regional Planning Guidance
Table 10 presents the original RPG rate, before the extra commitments for the South East were added after the Sustainable Communities Plan.

Table 10: Annual RPG9 housebuilding rate for 2001-06, by South East county, before the Sustainable Communities Plan

County	Annual Average Rate
Berkshire	2,620
Buckinghamshire	3,210
East Sussex	2,290
Hampshire	6,550
Kent	5,700
Oxfordshire	2,430
Surrey	2,360
West Sussex	2,890
Total	28,050

Sustainable Communities Plan (2003-2031)
The wording in the Sustainable Communities Plan is quite vague; it simply states that: 'London and the Growth Areas [Thames Gateway, Milton Keynes-South Midlands, London-Stansted-Cambridge and Ashford] have the potential to accommodate an additional 200,000 homes above those currently planned in regional planning guidance' (ODPM, 2003). As the growth areas cross different regional boundaries and RPGs, it is difficult to unpick what this means for each individual region.

SEERA are working on an assumption that the South East's commitments under the Sustainable Communities Plan equate to an extra 1,500 homes a year. This would bring the revised RPG figure up to 29,500.

Bramley (2005) has criticised this, arguing that SEERA should have accounted for an extra 4,000 homes a year, not 1,500. Under the Sustainable Communities Plan, Ashford is due to deliver an additional 31,000 dwellings, which over the 28 years of the plan equates to 1,100 dwellings a year. Parts of the Thames Gateway and the Milton Keynes-South Midlands growth areas are also in the South East. Bramley (2005) argues that these will demand housebuilding figures 'at least as big again' as those for Ashford. Therefore he suggests an extra 4,000 dwellings should have been added to the 28,050 figure, which would bring the total to 32,000.

The South East Plan

SEERA officials' recommendations
SEERA commissioned Anglia Polytechnic University to model two projections to establish a range of population, household and dwelling growth for the purposes of testing spatial options in the South East Plan. One is based on long term (ten-year) migration assumptions, the other on short-term (five-year) migration assumptions.

Their work has translated into a projected household increase of between 724,000 and 866,000 households in the South East during the period 2001-02 to 2026-27 (one-third of which results from net in-migration into the region, the remainder from internally generated needs). This would translate into an annual increase of between 28,960 and 34,640.

Additional factors:

■ Backlog was estimated to be around 29,000 households in 2001, with the aspiration to clear this within 20 years.

■ Shortfall against previous targets during the 1990s would also need to be addressed.

■ To replace existing poor quality stock in the region the officials estimated that 5,000 dwellings would be required over the planning period.

■ No allowance was made for overspill from London if the capital did not meet its own targets.

The SEERA Regional Planning Committee recommended that three levels of housing growth should be consulted on for the South East Plan:

■ 29,500 (i.e. current government target);

■ 32,000;

■ 36,000.

It is unclear how these three figures account for the different demographic projections, and assumptions about clearing any backlog, covering any shortfall against previous targets or replacing existing stock. For example, the high end of the demographic projections plus the backlog aspiration would equal 37,540 on its own – above the highest recommendation of 36,000.

The response of Assembly Members
The Assembly voted to reject the three options put forward by the Regional Planning Committee. Instead they decided to consult on three different options, with the explanation for these options as provided in the public questionnaire set out in brackets below:[12]

- 25,500 (build fewer homes each year to match the average we achieved over the past five years);

- 28,000 (build new homes at approximately the same level that we achieved last year);

- 32,000 (build more new homes to meet the level that some experts say we will need in the future).

The results of the public consultation are due very soon.

Bramley's (2005) figures for the South East

Bramley arrives at a much higher figure for housebuilding in the South East through two different approaches. His first approach assumes significant overspill from London to the South East based on the unlikelihood that the capital will build as many houses as might be needed. The result is a figure of 41,000 as set out below:

$$
\begin{array}{ll}
\text{Increase in households} = & 32,400 \\
\text{London's overspill} \quad = & 8,640 \\
\textbf{Total} \qquad\qquad = & \textbf{41,040}
\end{array}
$$

The increase in households is drawn from the 2004 projections. These projections identify an increase in the number of households in the South East between 2001 and 2011 to be 320,400, or 30,240 per year.

Bramley (2005) also argues that London is unlikely to build enough dwellings to meet the annual household increase of 48,300 between 2001-2011, projected in the ONS 2004 interim projections. Housebuilding in London has only averaged 15,000 over the last decade, with current provision at 23,920. Bramley argues that with the new growth areas coming on line, London may be able to build the 30,000 dwellings a year London Plan target. This would still leave a shortfall of 18,000 households a year. As the South East absorbs 48 per cent of all out-migrants from London to the Greater South East (where such 'displaced' households are more likely to live for employment reasons), the potential overspill to the South East is 8,640.

It should be noted, however, that the London authorities provide a different view on the level of future household growth. They cite a figure of 34,000 a year, and also predict London will soon increase output to 30,000 dwellings a year. Under this calculation, the potential overspill to the South East is likely to be closer to 2,000. This then is another area of significant uncertainty in the debate on housing numbers.

Bramley's second approach argues that 41,000 homes a year in the South East would contribute towards the Barker (2004) affordability agenda. Interestingly how-

---

12 www.southeast-ra.gov.uk/southeastplan/consultation/questionnaire.php

ever, and as previously noted, this is within a broader argument that Bramley (2005) develops that Barker (2004) has significantly overstated the level of new dwellings required to improve affordability by driving down the trend rate of growth of real house prices. Rather than Barker's (2004) overall figure of 140,000 additional new dwellings a year, Bramley (2005) suggests 59,000 will have the same effect. Regional breakdowns are not given for either figure. But again one is struck by the range of estimates being provided, in this case casting doubt on the robustness of the modelling that would seem to be required to set national and regional affordability targets.

Appendix for chapter 4 – Transport: keeping the South East moving

Road user charging modelling assumptions

ippr commissioned Imperial College to conduct some modelling on the effects of a national congestion charging scheme, if it were introduced on all roads throughout England in 2010. The forecasts were made using a computer model of England's transport system, first developed for the Independent Transport Commission (Glaister and Graham, 2003). The model differentiates between the nine English Government Office regions, different area types from metropolitan to rural, different road types from motorway to unclassified and different times of the day and week. It distinguishes five different types of road vehicle.

The model is based on year 2000 traffic data supplied by the Department for Transport, projected to 2010, and is consistent with the Government's forecast for overall traffic growth of 20 to 25 per cent. It uses the same assumptions as the Department for Transport in its own national transport model that, by 2010, real fuel prices will have fallen by 12 per cent and fuel efficiency will have improved such that average fuel costs per km will have fallen by 30 per cent (DfT, 2005). Beyond 2010 traffic forecasts are speculative. To ensure the modelling was robust, the scenarios tested therefore only look out to 2010.

Two different scenarios for congestion charging in 2010 were tested: 1. Revenue raising, in which congestion charges are added to existing motoring costs and 2. Revenue neutral, whereby congestion charging is offset by cuts in fuel tax so that no net extra revenue is raised overall.

Congestion charges in the model are set according to estimates of the time costs of congestion, with an additional amount for the environmental costs of carbon dioxide emissions, which vary by area, road type and time period. The modelling uses a long run price elasticity of traffic with respect to price of 0.3 which assumes that for every ten per cent increase in price there is a three per cent reduction in traffic. The forecasts should be taken as illustrative of the likely direction and magnitude of changes rather than as precise measurements.

South East Committees and Regional Boards

South East Planning Committee
The role of the South East Planning Committee is to advise the Regional Assembly on matters relating to the Assembly's role as the Regional Planning Body for the South East. The Regional Assembly is responsible for developing the Regional Spatial Strategy. The Planning Committee has 25 members who are appointed at the Assembly's annual

meeting. The Chair of the Planning Committee is currently the Leader of Oxfordshire County Council. The Committee membership reflects the balance on the Assembly between local government and social, environmental and economic partners. There are 16 local authority members, one from town and parish councils, four from the social/environmental partners and four from the economic partners. Up to ten members of the Regional Planning Committee can be non-Assembly Members nominated according to their knowledge and experience.

South East Regional Housing Board
The South East Regional Housing Board was set up following publication of the Government's Sustainable Communities Plan in February 2003. The Board takes specific responsibility for the preparation of the Regional Housing Strategy for the South East, as the basis to inform ministers on strategic housing investment priorities within the region. The seven board members are largely senior officials drawn from SEERA and GOSE. The Chair of the Regional Housing Board is the Regional Director at GOSE. In addition, the Regional Housing Board has seven non-executive members who are Assembly Members. The Regional Housing Board currently sits within GOSE.

Experimental South East Transport Board
Along with Yorkshire and Humberside, the South East has been one of the regions to set up an Experimental South East Transport Board. It was set up to assess some of the following:

■ The alignment between the Regional Spatial Strategy, the Regional Transport Strategy, the Regional Economic Strategy and the Regional Housing Strategy and any relevant national policies and priorities (including PSA targets);

■ How best to allocate hypothetical regional budgets covering capital and current/ revenue expenditure on Local Transport and on Highways Agency roads of regional importance;

■ Alternative sets of allocations on the assumption that there is freedom to transfer funds between all expenditure streams, including between capital and current spending; and identify any significant issues arising in respect of rail;

■ To identify any lessons for the development of the Regional Spatial Strategy and other regional strategies and for Local Transport Plans (SEERA, 2004b).

The 12 board members of the Experimental South East Transport Board reflected the balance on the Assembly between local government and social, environmental and economic partners. The Chair of the Experimental South East Transport Board has been the Director of Transport at GOSE. The board has been supported by an Officers Group made up of ten senior officials drawn from the South East authorities and agencies.